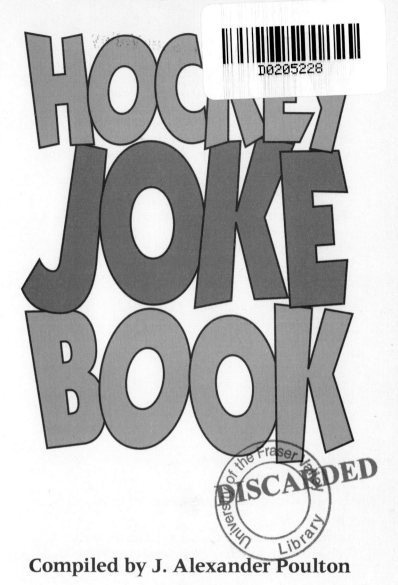

HOCKEY JOKE BOOK

Compiled by J. Alexander Poulton

OVER
TIME
BOOKS

© 2009 by OverTime Books
First printed in 2009 10 9 8 7 6 5 4 3
Printed in Canada

The Publisher: OverTime Books is an imprint of Éditions de la Montagne Verte
The Website: www.overtimebooks.com

Library and Archives Canada Cataloguing in Publication

Poulton, J. Alexander (Jay Alexander), 1977–
        Hockey joke book / J. Alexander Poulton.

        ISBN 978-1-897277-40-9

        1. Hockey—Canada—Humor. 2. National Hockey League—Humor. I. Title.

PN6231.H54P69 2009   C818'.602   C2009-903555-3

Project Director: J. Alexander Poulton
Project Editor: Brian Crane
Cover Illustration: Roger Garcia

We acknowledge the financial support of the Government of Canada through the Book Publishing Industry Development Program for our publishing activities.

Canadian   Patrimoine
Heritage   canadien

PC: 1

Contents

Dedication

To the deadline

Introduction

Hockey's True Beginnings?

Hockey is thought to have originated in ancient Greece. During their winter break, many Greeks would take vacations up north in what is today Sweden and Russia. When the lakes froze over, the Greeks would undress down to their sandals (unless it was dangerously cold) and play a game strikingly similar to hockey. The local population was intrigued by this sport and adopted it as their own. However, because they were not as crazy, they decided to keep their clothes on while playing.

Hockey is a serious sport, but as with all things serious, sometimes you just have to have a laugh. The jokes, puns, anecdotes and true (sometimes) stories in the following pages are an attempt to lighten the mood in a sport that can take itself a little too seriously. After all, it's just a game.

The range of jokes out there in the world reflects just how deep the sport has settled into our popular culture, even to the point where the 2008 Republican nominee for Vice-President of the United States used the sport's tough image to help her in her campaign. The jokes ended up back-firing, and she lost her bid. But hockey was once again at the front of everyone's attention in North America. Here's an example of Palin jokes from that memorable campaign.

Q: "What's the difference between a hockey mom and a pit bull?

A: Lipstick!

Funny right? Well, this is a joke that keeps on giving. There are tons of way it could go. Some alternate answers?

A: 5 million dollars' worth of lipstick on the tax-payers' tab!

A: Pit bulls had to evolve; politicians and hockey moms were poofed onto the earth by God.

A: A pit bull isn't going to track you down and throw you in Gitmo after we win in November. We'll see who's laughing then, you smart-ass terrorist.

A: One barks at outsiders; the other is a pit bull.

Hockey has gone global, and so have the jokes. Once it was only Canadians and a few Americans who were the butt of all the jokes, but hockey humour knows no boundaries. For example, here is one of my personal favourites:

Q: How do you get European skaters into the corners?

A: Start a fight at centre ice!

Here's another one:

Q: How do Russians celebrate a Stanley Cup victory?

A: They go into town and get smashed.

As much as possible, I have tried to spread the humour around and to make both sexes and many cultures the butt of the jokes. This way, everyone can feel like they have been equally insulted.

One of the most prevalent types of joke and anecdote is player and team humour. The rivalry between different teams in the decades since professional hockey began has led to such a plethora of jokes that it has been almost impossible to fit everything into this book. Being from Montréal, Canada, I naturally have my share of Toronto Maple Leaf jokes. For example:

Q: Why doesn't Hamilton have an NHL team?

A: Because then Toronto would want one.

I have tried to put aside my bias for the Canadiens and take every opportunity to skewer all teams and players. Although, for some reason, there seem to be a lot of Sean Avery jokes.

So, whether you are looking for a joke about your favourite team or player or just about two idiots out on the ice, you will find one in this book. We have run the gamut of the hockey culture, from hockey moms to wise-arse hockey kids, and pulled out its funniest, crudest, rudest, most gut-wrenching jokes. Remember: hockey is just a sport, and when you take something so seriously for most of your life, it's good to just sit back and have a laugh. I did. Enjoy.

Chapter One

Hosers Love Hockey

"Hockey captures the essence of Canadian experience in the New World. In a land so inescapably and inhospitably cold, hockey is the chance of life and an affirmation that despite the deathly chill of winter we are alive."

— *Stephen Leacock*

"In English-speaking Canada, hockey sometimes seems to be the sole assurance that we have a culture. That is something never in question in Québec."

–*Rick Saluting, playwright, in the Preface to* Les Canadiens

"Canadian hockey has been carried to all parts of the world, usually on a stretcher."

–*Eric Nichol and Dave More in their 1978 book,*
The Joy of Hockey

"This is the only country in the world where, in thousands of gardens, tomato plants are held up with broken hockey sticks. This is a unique Canadian happening."

—Robert F. Harney, former director of the
Multicultural History Society of Ontario

"Canada is made up of half-failed hockey players—and half women—all of us involved in a shared delusion, whether in a church league in Toronto or the Wild Goose League in Saskatchewan."

—Dick Beddoes, sports writer

"Canadians can't play baseball because baseball is a summer game, and Canada has no summer. Canadians should stick to their native sports, namely, hockey and pelt trapping."

—Jimmy Breslin, American writer, commenting on singer
Mary O'Dowd's forgetting the words to the U.S. national
anthem at a Toronto Blue Jays–New York Yankees game

Graffiti on an Edmonton wall:
JESUS SAVES!

Gretzky gets the rebound,

He shoots, he scores!

Hockey Night in Canada?

Play-by-play announcer in a game between the Vancouver Canucks and the Toronto Maple Leafs:

"And here comes the Leafs' Grabovski, with a pass to Antropov, then it's to Kulemin. Oh, the Canucks' Hordichuk grabs the puck, then shoots a quick pass to Demitra, over to Bieska, to the point to Ohlund. The block, it's picked up by the Leafs, and here comes Blake...Blake? What kind of ridiculous name is Blake for a hockey player?"

Q: How many Canadians does it take to screw in a light bulb?

A: No one knows. They are all too busy playing hockey to care about some stupid light bulb.

Q: Why are the Leafs like Canada Post?

A: The both wear uniforms and don't deliver!

The Official Canadian Temperature Conversion Chart!

50°F (10°C)

New Yorkers try to turn on the heat.

Canadians plant gardens.

40°F (4.4°C)

Californians shiver uncontrollably.

Canadians sunbathe.

35°F (1.6°C)

Italian cars won't start.

Canadians drive with the windows down.

32°F (0°C)

Distilled water freezes.

Canadian water gets thicker.

0°F (–17.9°C)

New York City landlords finally turn on the heat.

Canadians have the last cookout of the season.

–40°F (–40°C)

Hollywood disintegrates.

Canadians rent some videos.

–60°F (–51°C)

Mount St. Helens freezes.

Canadian Girl Guides sell cookies door to door.

–100°F (–73°C)

Santa Claus abandons the North Pole.

Canadians pull down their earflaps.

–173°F (–114°C)

Ethyl alcohol freezes.

Canadians get frustrated when they can't thaw the keg.

−460°F (−273°C)

Absolute zero; all atomic motion stops.

Canadians start saying, "Cold, eh?"

−500°F (−295°C)

Hell freezes over.

The Toronto Maple Leafs win the Stanley Cup.

Cup Final: Toronto versus Montréal

It's Game Seven of the Stanley Cup final, Toronto versus Montréal, and a man makes his way to his seat, right down at centre ice. He sits down and notices that the next seat is empty. He leans over and asks his neighbour if someone will be sitting there.

"No," he replied, "that seat shall be empty."

"That is incredible! Who in their right mind would give up a seat like this and miss the final game of the playoffs?!"

The neighbour says, "Well, actually, that seat belonged to my wife; she passed away, and this is the first game we haven't been to together since we were married in 1967."

"Oh, I am so sorry. You couldn't find anyone who would want to take this seat?"

"No," the man said. "They are all at her funeral!"

The French Love Hockey

"How did the first Frenchman get to Toronto?"

"A bunch of them were playing hockey on the frozen St. Lawrence, and one got a breakaway."

Québec Sports

Gilles Duceppe retired from public life and moved to Spain to get away from it all. Once settled, he got into a conversation with his neighbour, who turned out to be as opinionated and outspoken as Duceppe.

The neighbour exclaimed, "So, you come from Québec. I understand hockey is the most popular sport in Québec. In France, we find it barbaric."

"Madame," said Duceppe. "I am surprised by your words. After all, in your country the most popular sport is bullfighting. Québecers find that sport more than barbaric. And you also expressed that hockey is the most popular sport in Québec. You are wrong on both accounts madam. Hockey is not Québec's most popular sport—revolting is."

Mom Beer

A Canadian hockey player is walking down the street with a case of beer under his arm.

His friend, Doug, stops him and asks, "Hey Bob! Whacha get the case of beer for?"

"I got it for my wife, eh," answers Bob.

"Oh!" exclaims Doug. "Good trade."

Oh, How Montréalers Love Hockey!!

Bill Shankly, the late, legendary Liverpool FC manager, reputedly said, "Some people believe football (soccer) is a matter of life and death. I'm very disappointed with that attitude. I can assure you it is much, much more important than that." Well, it seems that Europeans are not the only ones who are mad about a sport. A Canadian man, more specifically, a Montréal hockey fan, appears to think the same way about hockey.

This particular Montréaler has put up a gravestone every time his team loses a major game. A Canadiens fan, Pierre Gaston, 52, has so far erected more than 20 of them in a local field. He says grave mistakes can only be marked by a gravestone, which he uses to bury his hopes and dreams, near his home in the southwest borough of Montréal.

Gaston said, "Instead of enjoying a celebration, I felt like I was at a funeral, so I spent the day carving out my fury on a stone."

Newbie Hockey Mom

Michael: My brother's away training to be on the provincial hockey team.

John: Lucky thing! He must be quite grown up now.

Michael: Yes. He wrote the other day saying he'd grown another foot, so my mom is knitting him an extra sock.

St. John's, Newfoundland, news anchor: "There was a terrible tragedy down at the local hockey pond. They all drowned during spring training."

Hockey versus the NRA

We will explain the appeal of hockey to you, if you Americans can explain the appeal of the National Rifle Association to us!

Newfie Hockey

"I've been playing hockey professionally for five years, now. Of course, my father was dead-set against my taking up the game at all. He wanted me to be a fisherman. In fact, he offered me $10,000 not to train."

"Really," said his friend. "What did you do with the money?"

In Canada we have two seasons: six months of winter and six months of poor hockey weather.

If Canada didn't have hockey, there'd be no culture at all.

Canadian New Year's Dinner

As in many Canadian homes on New Year's Day, my wife and I faced the annual conflict over what was more important: the Canadian Junior Games on television or New Year's Eve dinner. To keep peace, I ate dinner with the rest of the family and even lingered for some pleasant after-dinner conversation before retiring to the family room to turn on the game.

Several minutes later, my wife came downstairs and graciously brought a cold drink for me. She smiled, kissed me on the cheek and asked what the score was. I told her it was the end of the second period and that the score was still nothing to nothing.

"See?" she said. "You didn't miss a thing."

Hockey Love

Two women are talking. "You know," says one. "Most Canadian men think the best way to end an argument is to make love."

"Well," says the other. "That will certainly revolutionize the National Hockey League."

Q: Why is the NHL Hall of Fame in Toronto?

A: Because it's the only way they can see the Cup.

Céline Dion is on the verge of buying the Montréal Canadiens. Because she wants to ruin more than just music.

Dallas centre Mike Modano broke Phil Housley's NHL record for career points by an American-born player. He earned seven. Being the best American hockey player is almost as cool as being the best Canadian baseball player.

NHL MasterCard commercial

Season Tickets: $1240

Montréal Canadiens Jersey: $120

Canadiens Playoff Tickets: $500

Seeing the Canadiens eliminate the Toronto Maple Leafs yet again: PRICELESS

A True Canadian

A Canadian is someone who drinks Brazilian coffee from an English teacup and munches a French pastry while sitting on his Danish furniture, having just come home from an Italian movie in his German car on a Saturday night, to watch Europeans play in the NHL. He then picks up his Japanese pen and writes to his Member of Parliament to complain about the American takeover of the Canadian publishing business.

Americans: Will jabber on incessantly about football, baseball and basketball.

Brits: Will jabber on incessantly about cricket, soccer and rugby.

Canadians: Will jabber on incessantly about hockey, hockey, hockey, hockey and how they beat the Americans once, playing baseball.

You Know You're From Canada When...

❏ The local paper covers national and international headlines on two pages, but the hockey news requires six pages.

❏ You perk up when you hear the theme from *Hockey Night in Canada*.

❏ You bring a portable TV on a camping trip, so you don't miss *Hockey Night*.

❏ You know who Foster Hewitt is.

❏ Complete the phrase: "The good old ____ game is the best ____ you can ____."

❏ Your Saturday nights in the Atlantic provinces include eating beans and brown bread as you watch *Hockey Night in Canada*.

❏ The municipality buys a Zamboni before buying a bus.

❏ You remember a time when the NHL had only two Canadian teams.

❏ You hate the Leafs.

❑ You are surrounded by hundreds of huge, horribly frigid lakes.

A young Newfoundland-born player is drafted by the Habs and is ready to attend his first training camp.

"How will I get by?" he asks his father. "I don't speak French."

"Just speak slow," the old man says." They understand you when you do that."

As the young man shows up at camp he walks up to another rookie and says, "Hi…my…name…is… John."

The other fella says, "Hi…my…name…is…Mark."

"Where…are…you…from?"

"New…found…land"

"Me…too"

"If…we're…both…from…the…Rock…then…why… are…we…wasting… our…time…speaking…French?"

Canada's worst air disaster occurred earlier this morning, when a small plane carrying 12 hockey players crashed into a cemetery in central Newfoundland. Newfie search-and-rescue workers have recovered 825 bodies, so far, and expect that number to climb as digging continues into the evening.

A Day of Golf with Mother Nature

Andre Kostitsyn of the Montréal Canadiens and Mikhail Grabovski of the Toronto Maple Leafs were out playing golf one beautiful day. After hitting their tee shots, both noticed that neither was even close to the fairway. One hit the ball way left, the other hit his way right. They decided that because the shots were so bad, they'd just meet up at the hole.

So Kostitsyn went off and looked and looked and finally found his ball sitting down deep in a field of beautiful buttercups. He promptly pulled out his seven-iron and started whacking away. Buttercups flew everywhere, but the ball wouldn't come out.

Well, finally Mother Nature got mad.

She came up from the ground and said to the man, "I've created this beautiful field of buttercups, and you have no respect for them at all. Now they are ruined. I'm going to have to punish you. Because these are buttercups, your punishment is that you cannot have butter for a year."

Kostitsyn started to laugh and went back to whacking at the buttercups.

Mother Nature said, "Hey, this is no laughing matter. What do you find so funny?"

The man looked up and said, "Grabovski is over on the other side in the pussy willows."

You Might Be a Canadian Hockey Lover If:

❑ someone asks how old your child is and you reply "Minor Atom"

❑ your odometer hits 100,000 kilometres in the arena parking lot

❑ it's just as dark outside when you leave the arena as when you arrived

❑ you convince people that practice Sunday mornings at 6:00 AM isn't really that bad

❑ people you don't know call you by your name at arenas

❑ it's so cold outside, starting the car would take longer than the trip to Timmy's, so you break down and drink the arena vending-machine coffee

❑ said vending machine coffee tastes good (because any flipping coffee tastes good at 6:00 AM!)

❑ you know where the warm seats (relatively speaking) are in every local rink

❑ you keep different types of hockey tape in your purse

❑ you keep track of time by skate sharpenings

❑ you wake up two hours early to shovel the driveway, so you'll get to the game or to practice on time, almost

❑ that glove smell no longer induces vomiting

❑ you know which arenas have slightly-above-freezing water in the washrooms, and you know which washrooms actually have soap

- ❏ you know whose turn it is to make the coffee run
- ❏ no one knows whose turn it is, and no one cares, because it all evens out
- ❏ you can tell the difference between the smell of laces and the smell of gloves
- ❏ a stranger stops you at the grocery store and asks, "Don't you work at the rink?"
- ❏ your holiday schedule is planned around games
- ❏ you see your friends at the arena more often than anywhere else
- ❏ the kids buy into your line about shovelling being good for their backhand shots
- ❏ you arrange to meet relatives at the arena
- ❏ you remember the rink you were in when your girlfriend called to tell you she was pregnant
- ❏ you remember the rink where your child was conceived (oops, was that my inside voice?)
- ❏ you know what rinks have amenities for grand-parents (viewing rooms and heat lamps!)
- ❏ despite all the hassles, you jump out of bed quicker for games and practices than anything else
- ❏ you don't think we're crazy for doing it week after week, month after month, year after year

---

Chapter Two

Players We Love And a Few We Hate

The Greatest One

A young hockey-loving kid dies and goes to heaven, where he meets St. Peter at the Pearly Gates.

"Do you want to join the Good Guys in heaven," asks St. Peter, "or the Bad Guys?"

"The Good Guys, of course," says the kid.

St. Peter shows him the way. Just then, one of the Good Guys appears, pushing everybody out of the way, stick-handling a puck through the crowd.

"If that bully is one of the Good Guys, what are the Bad Guys like?" asks the kid.

"I know what you're thinking," answers St. Peter. "But he's not a Bad Guy, only God. Sometimes he likes to pretend he's Wayne Gretzky."

The Rocket

Legendary French sports broadcaster Rene Lecavalier liked to tell the story that if a popularity vote were to be taken in Québec between the Pope and Maurice "Rocket" Richard, Richard would be the easy winner, because the Pope couldn't skate like the Rocket!

Duh!

Sean Avery gets off the ice on his first game back after taking a vicious hit. He motions to the trainer for attention and shouts that his rib is cracked. The trainer states that he shouldn't shout things like that. "You want to appear invincible and never let the other team know where you hurt, or they will target you there."

"But my ribs are cracked!" pleads Avery.

"You need to redirect it. State that you need another stick or that your skate is dull, and when I come over, tell me what you really need."

After returning to action several weeks later, Avery takes a stick to the face, he keeps his head high and skates over to the bench as if nothing happened, despite blood coming out of his eyes. He motions to the trainer and yells. "There is something wrong with my skates."

The guys all smile, knowing that Avery took on the advice. The trainer yells, "What's wrong with them?"

Avery yells back, "I can't see out of them!"

Watch my Back

Teemu Selanne and Chris Pronger accidentally walked into a gay bar. They had just sat, when a man walked up to Teemu and asked him to dance.

Horrified, he turned to Pronger and whispered, "Help me out of this!" So Pronger grabs the guy, slams him up against the wall and mumbles something menacingly into his face. Once let out of his clutches, the guy apologized and hurried away.

"Wow," Teemu says, "thanks. What did you say to him?" Prongs shrugged and replied, "Told him we're on our honeymoon."

Tough Choice

Brendan Shanahan was trying to choose which of his three girlfriends to marry, so he gave each one $5000 to see how she would spend it. The first spent hers on a makeover, clothes, a new hairdo, manicure, pedicure, the works. She tells Shanahan, "I spent the money, so I could look pretty for you, because I love you so much." The second one went out and bought new golf clubs, a CD player, a television and a stereo. She gives them to Shanahan and says, "I bought these gifts for you with the money, because I love you so much." The third one takes the $5000 and invests it in the stock market, doubles her investment, returns the $5000 to Shanahan and reinvests the rest. She says, "I am investing the rest of the money for our future, because I love you so much." Shanahan thought long and hard about how each of the women spent the money and decided to marry the one with the biggest bra size.

Tattoo

A lady walks into a tattoo parlour. She's been told that the artist is the best. Being a *huge* Wayne Gretzky fan, she requests that he put Wayne's face on her right inner thigh. After an hour of work, the artist finishes and shows the lady his work.

"This doesn't look anything like Gretzky," she says.

So he takes out a picture of Wayne and compares them.

"See, they look just alike."

The lady does not agree. So the artist agrees to do Wayne on the other thigh for free.

She comes back the next day to have her left thigh done. He does the tattoo and excitedly shows it to her.

"This one doesn't look like Wayne Gretzky, either!" she says.

The artist insists that this one is identical to the picture of Wayne that she brought. To solve the debate, the artist calls his friend, a huge hockey fan, over to decide. The friend comes over and the lady lifts her dress to show the tattoos.

"Hmmm, I'm not sure who the wingers are, but the centre is definitely Lanny McDonald."

Smart Dog

A man walks into a Montréal bar with a dog. The bartender says, "You can't bring that dog in here."

"You don't understand," says the man. "This is no regular dog. He can talk."

"Listen, pal," says the bartender. "If that dog can talk, I'll give you a hundred bucks."

The man puts the dog on a stool and asks him, "What's on top of a house?"

"Roof!"

"Right. And what's on the outside of a tree?"

"Bark!"

"And who's the greatest hockey player of all time?"

"Howe!"

"I guess you've heard enough," says the man. "I'll take the hundred in twenties."

The bartender is furious. "Listen, pal," he says, "get out of here before I belt you."

As soon as they're on the street, the dog turns to the man and says, "Do you think I should have said 'Richard'?"

Old Timer

Old Dave had been retired from the game for many years, but he still liked to tell people how good he'd once been.

"They still remember me, you know," he said. "Only yesterday, when I was at the players' entrance, there were lots of press photographers lining up to take my picture."

"Really?" said a disbelieving listener.

"Yes. And if you don't believe me, ask Sidney Crosby—he was standing right next to me."

One Man!

Alexander Ovechkin went into the Washington changing room, to find his teammates looking glum. "What's up?" he asked.

They replied: "We're having trouble getting motivated for this game—it's only Toronto."

Ovechkin said: "I think I can beat them by myself—you go to the bar and relax."

So Ovechkin went and played Toronto by himself. After a few drinks, the rest of the team wondered how the game was going, so they asked the bartender to turn on the TV. The score read: "Washington 1, Toronto 0 (Ovechkin 10th min, 1st period)." After several more drinks, they checked the final score on the TV. It said, "Washington 1 Toronto 1 (Finger 19th min, 3rd period)." They couldn't believe that Ovechkin had single-handedly pulled a draw against Toronto, so they rushed to the stadium to congratulate him. Instead, he was sitting with his head in his hands and wailing: "I've let you down."

Don't be silly," they said. "You got a draw against Toronto—and they only scored at the very end."

"No, no, " he cried, "I have, I've let you down! Stupid, stupid, stupid! I got sent off after 12 minutes!"

Hey Johnny!

The great hockey player Jim 'Big Hands' O'Reilly was walking down the street. "I recognize that man," said a passerby. "But what's his name?"

"That's Big Hands," replied another passerby.

"Oh, really?" said the other.

"No, O'Reilly."

Ugly

Lyle Odelein and Gino Odjick are sitting in a dorm talking about girls. Odelein says to the other, "I never get lucky. I'm just too ugly."

Odjick says, "No man, you just need to go to where I live. Back home, girls don't even care what you look like."

Odelein says, "Well, let's go!" They take the bus and get off in Odjick's neighbourhood. They start walking down the street, and Odelein turns and sees this beautiful woman across the street, curling her finger toward herself and saying, "Come here." Odelein turns to Odjick and says, "You were right. I'll meet up with you later. See ya!"

So he runs across the street and starts following the woman. She disappears for a brief moment around the bend of a building and then reappears signalling with her finger, "Come here."

He continues to follow her. She disappears behind another building, then reappears once again, still curling her finger, "Come here." Finally, he sees her at the top of an apartment's stairs. One last time, she curls her finger, "Come here."

Odelein goes up the stairs and walks into the apartment, which is pitch dark. He closes the door behind him, and suddenly the lights turn on. There, he sees the woman pointing at three kids, saying, "I told you if you were bad, I was going to bring you the Boogie Man!"

Three Stars

Maurice "the Rocket" Richard is interviewed on *Hockey Night in Canada* as the guest judge for the three stars selection.

"For de firs star, I pick Guy Lafleur. He skate like de wind up and down da wing, 'e score and 'ave an assist, anudder great game."

"For de secon star, I pick my liddle broder, the pocket rocket, Henri Richard. He 'ave a great game, he assist and he iz my liddle broder."

"And for de turd star, I pick dat g*ddamn Bobby Orr. If it wern for 'is three goal and two assist, we woulda won da f***ing game."

Trade

Kevin Lowe went to a movie with Dwayne Roloson. Halfway through the movie, Roloson said he was hungry and was going to get some popcorn and nachos.

Kevin Lowe told him that he had to go to the washroom and said he would pick up the snacks. So off he went.

After going to the bathroom, he bought an extra-large order of nachos and a super tub of popcorn. On his way back, he bumped into Darryl Sutter, who said, "Wow, Kevin, you must be pretty hungry."

Lowe immediately said, "No, you don't under-stand—I got this for Dwayne Roloson."

To which Sutter replied, "Awesome! That's way more than you got for Ryan Smyth."

Lucky Looney

Jarome Iginla takes a tour of the Hockey Hall of Fame one day and isn't feeling too good about him-self, for some reason. He comes across "the Loonie" that had been under the ice when Canada won Olympic Gold. He looks at it intently and says, "I wish I could be at least one percent better at hockey." The next game the Calgary Flames play, he plays so perfectly that none of the refs can find one thing to give him a penalty for.

After the game, the team goes to the pub and Miikka Kiprusoff asks Iginla what happened to make him so immune to the refs. Iginla tells him about the Loonie. One day, not long after that, Kiprusoff goes to see the Loonie. He stares at it intently and says, "I wish I could be at least one percent better at goaltending." The next game he plays, not a single puck gets by him. Better yet, every player on the opposing team that so much as taps him is given a penalty.

The team again goes to a pub, and when Kiprusoff is asked how he also became so invincible, he replies with Iginla's story of the Loonie. The Vancouver Canucks' Mats Sundin is nearby and overhears this. He then goes to see the Loonie. He thinks Iginla a fool to only ask for one percent, so he looks intently at the Loonie and says, "I wish I could be at least 100 percent better at hockey." He smiles contently to himself and walks away. But then he sees his reflection in a glass display case and discovers that he's turned into Jarome Iginla.

Sean Avery was at home with a beautiful woman.

"Take off my shoes," she said.

Sean Avery obeyed.

"Now, take off my dress," she said.

Again, Sean Avery was happy to comply.

"Now, take off my stockings, my garter belt and my panties."

Sean Avery obeyed without saying a word.

"Now, take off my bra," said the woman, "and don't let me ever catch you wearing my clothes again!"

Avery Leaves Dallas

Sean Avery, who was suspended by the Dallas Stars, won't return to the team. Another team might pick him up, but only if they're allowed to call him "sloppy seconds."

The Stanley Cup champion Red Wings were honoured at the White House. Before they left, President Bush asked goalie Chris Osgood if he'd stand between him and the media.

Andreas Lilja of the Red Wings had an operation to take out his appendix. When fans heard that Detroit removed an unnecessary organ, many thought the Lions had moved.

Party

Wayne Gretzky was at a party at Brian Leetch's house. Gretzky took Leetch aside and said, "Hey, there are lots of beautiful women here. If I find a live one, can I use your extra bedroom?"

"I don't know," Leetch replied. "What about your wife?"

"Don't worry about it. I'll only be gone a few minutes. She'll never miss me."

"Probably not," Leetch said. "She borrowed the extra bedroom fifteen minutes ago."

Domi

Tie Domi's wife was getting irritated with how friendly he was being with the young girl across the street. One day she looked out the window to see Domi and the girl talking in her front yard. So, she picked up the phone and called the neighbour. "Tell my husband to get his ass across the street!" she demanded. The girl replied sweetly, "Ma'am, that's where he's been getting his ass for weeks."

Just Wrong

After again missing the playoffs, Mats Sundin and his wife went golfing. They are having a wonderful time, and Sundin has had a near-perfect game. The final hole, by far the most difficult, wraps around an old barn. With a terrible slice, Sundin puts the barn between his ball and the green. Knowing that getting around the barn will destroy his score, he begins to rant and rave. His wife, hating to see him ruin such a great afternoon, makes a suggestion.

"What if I were to hold the barn doors open? That way, you could send it right through the barn and onto the green."

Sundin thinks this over and decides that it will work. With his wife holding open the barn door, he lines up with the hole and gives the ball a terrific "whack"! The ball flies through the air and right into his wife's head, killing her instantly.

Months go by, Sundin mourning all the while. His friends, hating to see him in such a state, convince him to go golfing with them. They end up at the same course, and on the final hole, oddly enough, another terrible slice puts the old barn between his ball and the green. Again, Sundin begins to rant and rave at what this dilemma will do to his score. The friends, wanting to please him, make a suggestion.

"What if we were to hold open the barn doors? That way you could send it right through the barn onto the green."

"No," Sundin replies, "last time I did that, I got two over par."

Rural Game

When Chris Pronger first went to play junior hockey in a rural Canadian outpost, he asked one of the older players what they did for a good time. "We use the mule," the older player told him. Revolted, Pronger turned his thoughts to other activities. However, after time passed, and he got hornier and hornier, he could think of nothing else. Finally, Pronger accepted the fact the mule was all there was. So one night, he snuck out to the barn.

A little later, as Pronger was walking away from the mule, the older player came out to the barn.

"What the hell are you doing?" the older player asked.

Puzzled, Pronger replied, "I thought you said you use the mule for a good time."

"Yeah, but we usually ride him into town."

Father and Son

Upon taking his son to see his first NHL game Ryan Kesler asked him, "So how did you enjoy it?"

The little boy was quite excited but said that he had a question. "Why do some guys only fight, but you don't?"

Not wanting to look bad or afraid to his little boy, Kesler explained that it was a measure of his skill and intelligence. The ones that fought were actually quite dumb and couldn't do anything else. The ones that didn't fight were smarter and more skilled.

After a game against the Sens, Kesler asked his boy if enjoyed the game, and the boy said "Yes." Then he said, "Dad, is Chris Neil a dumb guy?"

"Yep, he's a dumb guy," Kesler stated angrily; Neil had scored in overtime.

"Well, lucky that he was on the ice against you, 'cause he just kept getting smarter and smarter."

Hunting Anyone

George Parros and Chris Pronger are out in the woods hunting, when George collapses. He doesn't seem to be breathing, and his eyes are glazed.

Chris takes out his phone and calls the emergency services. He gasps, "I think my friend is dead! What can I do?"

The operator says, "Calm down, I can help. First, let's make sure he's dead."

There is a silence, then a gunshot is heard. Back on the phone, Chris says: "Okay, now what?"

Fairy Tale

Guy Lafleur is walking along the roadside when he spots a small frog. The frog says "Kiss me, and I'll turn into a princess." Guy picks up the frog and puts it into his pocket. The frog says, "Didn't you hear me? Kiss me, and I'll turn into a princess."

Guy says, "I heard you, but at my age, I'd rather have a talking frog."

Pat Quinn probably knew he was going to get fired as coach of the Maple Leafs two weeks before the season ended: John Ferguson bought the entire team sets of new golf clubs.

NHL Chain Letter

This is a chain letter. Do not break the chain, or the National Hockey League will send Bob Probert to your house and break your face.

Hello.

My name is Gary Bettman, and I am commissioner of a struggling hockey empire based in the village of New York in a remote nation called the United States of America (and, for now, in some parts of a border country called Canada, although we are trying to fix that). Survival is not easy in my empire. Often it gets very cold outside, forcing its officers to flee to warmer places, like Hawaii or Southern Florida, to hold their winter survival meetings. Soon, they will run out of such places in their own country and will be forced to migrate to foreign places like the Costa del Sol.

Our plight grows more desperate by the day. Just this week, for instance, during a caviar break following my report that our empire's revenues have trebled in the '90s to about $14 billion because of expansion fees and several other forms of highway robbery that do not actually involve the use of a gun, it was noted that the governments of our teams in the Canadian colonies are still refusing to grant their team tax privileges and other pork barrel sustenance not available to the common folk.

Frankly, we are halfway to our wits' end trying to convince them to open their hearts and wallets, so that our empire can continue to grow and prosper without forcing us to open our own. How can we make them understand our plight? Why can they not understand that, though revenues in the wealthier outposts do range from

*$60–70 million US, the poorer must get by on merely $30–
40 million?*

*Desperate, we turn to you for help. Please send this letter
to five of your friends and ask each of them to send us $10
(US funds, no coins or stamps). They must, of course, send
copies to five of THEIR friends, with instructions to do the
same thing.*

*Or, if you really want to help, place a chessboard on your
web page and invite them to play a game. The first person
puts a drawing of a $1 bill on the first square, then sends
the actual money to us. Then each person in turn doubles
the number of dollars in the previous square. Won't that
be fun?*

*We beg you not to turn your back on our people—not
because it will hurt us but because dreadful things could
happen to you. Only a few years ago, someone broke one of
our earlier chains in Winnipeg, which we understand is in
Canada. Within months, their hockey outpost was blown
clear to Arizona, leaving their people huddled against an
October blizzard on the corner of Portage and Main uttering piteous cries—"TEEE-MU! TEE-MU!" They lamented
the way they'd ignored the warnings from another Canadian place called Ke-Bec that had also broken the chain.
The Ke-Bec legend is retold each year as our people gather
'round the liqueur table at our annual gatherings: the
Ke-Bec people watched one team disappear into Colorado
and, for their sins, have seen their other team of Flying
Frenchmen—now populated by foreigners—doomed to
finish in the cellar.*

Do not let this happen to you. Do not break the chain. Pick five of your richest friends and add links to our survival fund, named for one of our patron saints. Send all contributions to Fund Our Scam To Expand Revenue (FOSTER), NHL, New York. No receipts will be issued, so that we can save pennies otherwise wasted on stamps.

Hurry. We're running out of pâté.

Mikka Kiprusoff, the Flames goalie, was so upset about losing the Stanley Cup that he decided to commit suicide by jumping out in front of a bus. Unfortunately, it went through his legs.

Innocent Golf Game

After being eliminated from the playoffs (again!), Vincent Lecavalier and Martin St. Louis are hitting the links at their local golf and country club. Luckily, it's a beautiful day, and there's hardly anyone on the course. So they breeze through the holes. Up around the seventh tee, they spot the first people on the course other than themselves, two ladies, who, from the guys' perspective, are having trouble on the green. In fact, they've each five-putted it!

Lecavalier says "Christ. I hope they just had a bad hole, I don't want to follow these broads for the next 11 holes!" St. Louis then says, "Well, maybe I'll go talk to them, and maybe they'll let us pass. I'll be back in a sec."

So, he trots off to go and ask. But then, about 100 feet from the women, he stops, turns and runs away from them as fast as he can. When he comes back, he exclaims, "Jesus! That's my wife and my girl-friend! They're both here! Golfing together! I'm sorry, man, but I can't say anything to them. I'm liable to be killed if they saw me. How about you go ask them?"

Lecavalier concurs and trots off to ask the women if they can pass and get on with their game. Then he stops suddenly, spins around and runs back to his buddy in the same manner. "What's wrong? What's the matter?" St. Louis says.

"Same damn thing," Lecavalier replies.

Tough Rookie

Three NHL coaches were arguing over who had the toughest, gutsiest rookies that year.

Ken Hitchcock says, "Obviously mine are. Watch. Hey rookie, go start a scrap with Georges Laraque."

Predictably the rookie gets his butt kicked all over the ice, and Mr. Hitchcock says, "That took guts."

Joel Quenneville says, "That's nothing. Hey you, go take out the Zamboni." The player dutifully skates out to the Zamboni at full speed and splat! Zamboni 1, player 0.

Mr. Quenneville says, "That took guts!"

Scotty Bowman says, "I'll show you a kid with guts; watch this. Hey kid, I want you to go out and wash my car and then take my dog for a walk."

The rookie looks over and flatly states "Screw you!"

"That, gentlemen, took guts!"

Don Cherry Defined

Don Cherry is the most loved/hated man in Canada. He wears the most eye-catching/averting suits and makes the most outrageous/rage-provoking, humorous/banal comments. He was recently named the seventh-greatest Canadian of all time, ahead of lesser-talented public figures such as Margaret Atwood, Oscar Peterson and Emily Carr. He is particularly popular in Québec, where fans are so outraged by his inflammatory remarks that the ratings of "Coach's Corner" are higher than anywhere else in the country.

Want to know more?

Don Cherry:

- Was a loudmouth coach of the Boston Bruins, who wasn't afraid to say what was on his mind.
- Is the reason why 100 percent of the Canadian population watches *Hockey Night in Canada* on CBC.
- Likes to yell.
- Knows that Europeans are pansies for wearing protective visors.

- Was revealed by scientists to have a skull filled with hot air and an enormous inner ear.
- Can hear all of his own mindless rambling thoughts.
- Enjoys pointing out each and everyone of non-Canadian players' flaws.
- Has no problem calling European players gay, even though he is often seen in floral pattern suits and likes to kiss Doug Gilmour.

Wayne Gretzky Defined
- Is one of the league's greatest all-time stars.
- Led the league in scoring for 15 of his 20 years in the NHL.
- Holds more scoring titles than any other athlete except the National Basketball Association's Wilt Chamberlain.
- Holds 60 records.
- Is a good cover-story.
- Is believed by Morpheus to be "The One."
- Is the reason so many Canadians named their kids Wayne.

Alexander Ovechkin Defined
- Got a lifetime contract with a salary the size of the U.S. budget.

- Lost his front teeth because he was using them to open bottles of vodka all the time.
- Is always saying "Бухаем не по хуйне сегодня" ("I score goals, biatch.").
- Can do whatever the heck he wants.
- Falls down accidentally and a penalty is called on the nearest opposing player.
- Is the only living being who can simultaneously kick the ass of both Michael Phelps and Chuck Norris.
- Learned to speak English by watching *Sesame Street*. (Seriously, 100 percent true.)
- Many of his sayings are kept secret because of the Russian reversal law.

While he was sitting on the sundeck of the local Edmonton golf club, Morty was hit in the head with a ball. By the time the offending golfer had chased down his shot, Morty had an ice pack on his head and was ripping mad.

"I'm going to take you to court!" Morty screamed at the golfer. Upon noticing that the golfer was none other than the Flames' Jarome Iginla, Morty said, "I'll sue you for five million dollars!"

Distressed, Iginla said meekly, "I said 'FORE!'"

With a triumphant look, Morty announced, "I'll take it!"

Bad Lie

One beautiful Sunday morning, Michael Ryder and Dan Cleary, two Newfie NHL players, are out golfing. Ryder happens to slice his ball deep into a wooded ravine. Rather than taking the stroke and dropping the ball at an easier location, Ryder grabs his seven-iron and proceeds down the embankment into the ravine in search of his lost ball. The brush is quite thick, but Ryder searches meticulously and suddenly he spots something shiny. As he gets closer, he realizes that the shiny object is a seven-iron in the hands of a skeleton lying near an old golf ball. Ryder excitedly calls out to his golfing partner, "Hey Cleary, come here. I've got trouble down here."

Ryder comes running over to the edge of the ravine and calls out, "What's the matter?"

Ryder shouts back, "Throw me my eight-iron! You can't get out of here with a seven!"

Machine

On Vincent Lecavalier's answering machine: "Hi! This is Vinnie! If you are my parents, I already sent the money. If you are my agent, settle this thing about the money. If you are Dean Lombardi, I don't have enough money. If you are my friends, you owe me money. If you are a female, don't worry, I have plenty of money."

Gator

Ed Belfour goes into a bar (huge surprise), and the bartender tells him there is a standing offer for all patrons: free liquor to anyone who can pass a test. So Eddie asks what the test is.

"Well," the barkeep says, "First you drink an entire gallon of our home-brewed moonshine all at once, without stopping or throwing up. Second, we got a gator out back with a sore tooth, and somebody has to take it out. Third, we got a woman upstairs who has never had an orgasm, and you gotta go take care of her.

"Done," says Eddie arrogantly. "I can drink anything and still pull off miracles. You're on!"

So he grabs the moonshine, downs it in only a few gulps, then staggers outside, shrieking, "Here gator, gator, gator!"

The rest of the bar patrons hear roaring and thumping and the most god-awful hollering and thrashing about, then sudden silence. Eddie stumbles back into the bar, his shirt torn, bleeding from one eye and shouts, "Now where is that bitch with the sore tooth?!"

Rob Ray returned early from a road trip and went home to find his wife in bed with another man.

"What in the hell are you doing?" Matt screamed as he dropped his bags.

Unfazed, his wife turned to her lover and said, as she rolled her eyes, "See...I told you he was stupid."

Dany Heatley boarded a flight, sat down next to a gorgeous woman and noticed she was reading a manual about sexual statistics.

"Is that an interesting book?" he asked, with a sketchy smile.

"Why yes," she said. "It claims that, on average, American Indians have the longest penises, and Polish men's are the biggest in diameter. By the way, my name is Jill."

Dany replied, " Nice to meet you. I'm Tonto Kowalski."

Chapter Three

Humorous Quotes

Legendary Boston Bruins defenseman Bobby Orr was once asked why he always wore a protective cup but played without a hockey helmet.

His reply: "I can always get someone else to do my thinking for me!"

"When I was a kid, I prayed for enough talent to be a pro hockey player, but I forgot to say NHL, because they only gave me enough to make the minors."

–Don Cherry, hockey legend

"Three years ago, I couldn't spell author, now I are one."

–Don Cherry, after releasing his autobiography

"My face is my mask."

–Goaltender Lorne John "Gump" Worsley

"The only job worse is a javelin catcher at a track-and-field meet."

–Gump Worsley, legendary NHL goaltender

"There are three things we must do tonight, and that is shoot and pass."

–Bernie "Boom Boom" Geoffrion, to his teammates

"Hockey is a sport for white men. Basketball is a sport for black men. Golf is a sport for white men dressed like black pimps."

–Tiger Woods

"I looked like a big stiff on television. What a sobering experience. I always thought of myself as Nureyev on ice. But, on TV, I realized that I was a dump truck. I was an elephant on wheels."

–Montréal Canadiens goaltender Ken Dryden

When the NHL lured Gary Bettman away from the NBA and appointed him to serve as the league's commissioner, many of his colleagues worried about Bettman's profound lack of hockey experience.

"I gave Gary a hockey puck once," Orlando Magic GM Pat Williams joked at the time, "and he spent the rest of the day trying to open it."

"Until we get an apology, we're not going to win a game. We vow not to win until we get an apology from Bettman."

—Buffalo Sabres winger Dixon Ward

"The three people I would most like to have dinner with would be Jesus, George Strait and Tiger Woods."

—Carey Price, Montréal Canadiens goaltender

"I really couldn't hear anything," he said. "Were they talking bad about me? Like I said, I couldn't really hear anything. I had two Stanley Cup rings in my ears."

*—Patrick Roy, during the NHL playoffs in 2003,
when a reporter asked whether he was bothered
by an opposing player's nasty comments about him*

"Playing with Steve Guolla is like playing with myself."

—San Jose Sharks Jeff Friesen, on his linemate

"Every time I get injured, my wife ends up pregnant."

—Chicago Blackhawks Doug Wilson

"One road trip, we were stuck on the runway for two hours. The plane kept driving and driving until we arrived, and I realized that we were on a bus!"

*—In 1999, after a dozen years in the National Hockey
League, Glenn Healy found himself playing in the IHL with
the Chicago Wolves. The transition took some getting used to.*

"Only in America."

*—Miroslav Satan, on his frequently
mispronounced name (pronounced Sha-tan)*

"I'm hoping for a bench-clearing brawl during the
warm-up, so I can go out and grab his stick."

*—Ron Tugnutt on Gretzky's last game
in Canada against the Ottawa Senators*

"Man, that guy is ripped! I mean, I've got the
washboard stomach, too. It's just that mine has
about two months of laundry on top of it."

—Shawn Burr on Eric Lindros

"Part of the learning curve in Edmonton is learning to hate Calgary."

—Steve Smith, former Oilers defensemen

"I wouldn't urinate in his ear if his brain was on
fire!"

*—Bobby Hull, on a long-time Montréal Canadiens rival (no
word on which player that was)*

"Of course I am rooting for the players on the
Ducks...I even root for the guys on Vancouver. They
weren't the ones who ****ed me."

*—Toronto Maple Leaf General Manager
Brian Burke on following his former Ducks*

"Hockey belongs on the Cartoon Network, where a person can be pancaked by an ACME anvil, then expanded—accordion-style—back to full stature, without any lasting side effect."

—Steve Rushin, sportswriter

An American Express card belonging to the wife of legendary "Miracle on Ice" hockey coach Herb Brooks was once stolen. "I've never reported it," he later confessed, "because the guy is spending about $200 a month less than my wife did!"

Bobby Hull had a similar problem. "My wife made me a millionaire," he once explained. "I used to have three million."

"I don't know, and I don't care."

—Patrice Brisebois after being asked by a reporter
if he was playing so bad because of apathy or ignorance

"It would have been worse, if we hadn't blocked the kick after Toronto's second touchdown!"

—Detroit Red Wings captain Alex Delvecchio, one sorry
night in 1973, after he was asked to comment on the
team's 13–0 drubbing at the hands of the Toronto Maple Leafs.

"Ice hockey is a violent game. You take a stick and hit a puck, or anyone who has recently hit a puck."

—H.L. Mencken, journalist and satirist

Hockey Legend King Clancy to a doctor: "Maybe I'm not perfect, Doc, but I don't bury my mistakes like you do."

"He treats us like men. He lets us wear earrings."

—Martin Rucinsky on why he likes
head coach Michel Theirien

"When I look at the net, I don't see a goalie," NHL star Pavel Bure once remarked. Radek Dvorak was rather more modest. "When I look at the net," he said, "I see two or three goalies!"

In April 2000, Russia's *Pravda* newspaper reported that hockey star Pavel Bure had broken off his engagement to tennis player Anna Kournikova. The reason? He found her mother too meddlesome. "A wedding is not in my plans," Bure meekly explained. "At the moment, I love hockey more than anything."

"Hockey is the most fun you can have without taking your clothes off."

—Unknown

"I asked my old man if I could go ice-skating. He told me, 'Wait till it gets warmer.'"

—Rodney Dangerfield

"Getting cut in the face is a pain in the butt."

–Theoren Fleury

"A free agent is a contradiction in terms."

–Unknown

"I knew that it was going to be a wild game when a fight broke out in the middle of the national anthem."

–Unknown

"Does Dolly Parton sleep on her back?"

–John Tortorella, head coach of the NHL Tampa Bay Lightning, after dispatching the Philadelphia Flyers in the third round of the 2004 NHL playoffs, when asked whether he was nervous about coaching in his first Stanley Cup final series

"I don't live in the fast lane, I live in the off ramp."

–Fred Shero, Philadelphia Flyers head coach during the Broad Street Bully days

"It was easy for the Commies to hide. They just put the subs in the corner. Everybody knows Swedes don't go into corners."

–Don Cherry, after Soviet subs entered Swedish waters during the Cold War

"Today, the National Hockey League announced the end of a 300-day lockout. Yeah, that is the best news for a Canadian since Celine Dion moved to Las Vegas."

—Conan O'Brien

Quote from the movie *Slapshot*: "I was coaching in Omaha in 1948, and Eddie Shore sends me this guy who was a terrible mas***bator. He would get deliberate penalties so he could get over in the penalty box all by himself and damned if he wouldn't..."

"Ice hockey players can walk on water."

—Unknown

Gordie Howe was once asked what he liked best about star forward Mario Lemieux. Howe's reply? "His paycheque."

"You don't have enough talent to win on talent alone."

—Herb Brooks, 1980 US Olympic hockey coach

"I'm not dumb enough to be a goalie."

—Brett Hull

"We can't play stupid hockey, dumb hockey, greedy hockey, selfish hockey. We have to put the team ahead of our personal feelings."

–Terry Crisp, ex-coach of the Tampa Bay Lightning

"The only difference between this and Custer's last stand was Custer didn't have to look at the tape afterwards."

–Terry Crisp, ex-coach of the Tampa Bay Lightning,
after a 10–0 loss to the Calgary Flames

"I just tape four Tylenols to it."

– Edmonton's Boris Mironov, on playing with a sore ankle

"As always, I remain hopeful that Don Cherry won't be offered the same length contract."

– Broadcaster Ron MacLean,
on his four-year contract renewal

"A puck is a hard rubber disc that hockey players strike when they can't hit one another."

– Jimmy Cannon

"We get nose jobs all the time in the NHL, and we don't even have to go to the hospital."

– Brad Park

"By the age of 18, the average American has wit-
nessed 200,000 acts of violence on television, most
of them occurring during Game 1 of the NHL playoff
series."

– Steve Rushin

"Ice hockey is a form of disorderly conduct in
which the score is kept."

–Doug Larson

"I was a multi-millionaire from playing hockey.
Then I got divorced, and now I am a millionaire."

–Bobby Hull

"There are two types of forwards: scorers and
bangers. Scorers score and bangers bang."

–Ken Dryden

"You're playing worse every day and right now
you're playing like the middle of next week."

–Herb Brooks, 1980 US Olympic Hockey Coach

"People didn't know the difference between
a blue line and a clothesline."

*– Al Michaels, describing Americans' knowledge
of hockey prior to the "Miracle On Ice"*

"This is the only thing that has seen more parties than us."

—Steven Tyler, Aerosmith's lead singer, after admiring the Stanley Cup

"There are still two or three guys who aren't willing to pay the price to win a game. This is not Wal-Mart. There are no discounts in this league."

—San Jose Coach Ron Wilson

"Yeah, I'm cocky and I am arrogant. But that doesn't mean I'm not a nice person."

—Jeremy Roenick

"I was three-quarters down the list of guys I would be facing in my first game when I realized I was looking at our own roster."

— Glenn Healy, on playing in the minors

"It felt like a golf swing and my head was on the tee."

—Edmonton's Tyler Wright, on being clubbed by Joe Murphy

"I guess they respect my shot, because they were all ready at the blue line."

—Patrick Roy, on his attempt at the Edmonton Oilers empty net

"I had to pinch myself, seeing the grassy knoll and the book suppository building."

–Trevor Linden, on viewing the site of John F. Kennedy's assassination in Dallas.

"I know I'm not very popular on Long Island. I don't know who's less popular, me or Joey Buttafuoco."

–New York Islander General Manager Don Maloney

"He's a gutless puke, that's what Travis Green is. That's why he doesn't wear an Islander uniform anymore."

–Mike Milbury, on former Islander Travis Green and his hit on Kenny Jonsson

"We're looking forward to building the type of team the Rangers are able to buy."

–Phoenix General Manager Bobby Smith.

"I tried to talk my daughter out of going with a hockey player, but he's a good kid. He asked me if he could marry Carrie before he asked her. I said: 'You want to what?' I thought he was just going to ask for more ice time."

–Phil Esposito, on his daughter Carrie getting engaged to Alexander Selivanov

"I honestly believe some would have given up their left leg to stop a shot in the third period."

–Milan Gajic

"Hating the Toronto Maple Leafs is as Canadian as maple syrup, Tim Horton's and paying taxes."

–Unknown

Giving the red light a workout was never a concern while Hardy Astrom was in goal for Don Cherry's Colorado Rockies in 1979–80. "First practice in Colorado, we were working on breakout drills. I shoot the puck at Hardy from the far blue line, and it goes right through his legs. 'Fluke,' I figure, so I shoot another one. Right through his legs again. 'Next drill,' I said. Actually, Hardy was a nice guy, he just had a weakness with pucks."

–Don Cherry

Overheard

Female heckler to the Ref: "If you were my husband, you grey-haired bum, I'd give you poison."

Ref, loudly: "Lady, if I was your husband, I'd take it."

Joe Hall, an early NHL tough guy with the Montréal Canadiens, acted instinctively when a whistle sounded during a 1918 game between Montréal and

Ottawa. He quickly assumed a spot in the penalty box. "What did you give him a penalty for?" demanded Canadiens captain Newsy Lalonde of referee Marsh. When the ref claimed that he had called no infraction, Lalonde asked the same question of the judge of play. Again, his question was greeted with a shrug, so Lalonde told Hall to get out of the box. "Sorry about that, Newsy," Hall said, as he sheepishly returned to his position on the Canadiens defence. "Force of habit, I guess."

Although famous in the 1990s as a broadcaster, Harry Neale was for years a not particularly success- ful coach and then GM, mostly with the Canucks. During one astonishing losing streak, Neale remarked dryly, "We're losing at home, and we're losing on the road. My failure as a coach is that I can't think of anywhere else to play."

The dictatorial owner of the Leafs signed the first Swedish-trained played for the NHL, future Hall of Famer Borje Salming and not-so-successful winger Inge Hammarstrom. While Inge had skill and speed and grace, his play along the boards and in the corners was nervous at best and led Ballard to comment: "He could go into the corner with six eggs in his pocket and not break one."

A quirky left-handed goalie for Toronto and Washington, Mike Palmateer was as quick with a joke as he was with his glove. In the spring of 1979, the Leafs were facing the Montréal Canadiens in the quarterfinals. In the third game in the series, with Toronto trailing 2–0 in the series, Cam Connor of the Habs scored a lucky goal on his first shift of the game, 5 minutes and 25 seconds into the second overtime period. After the game, Palmateer declared: "That's one thing I can't do—stop someone who doesn't know what he's doing."

"I prefer the NHL style of hockey. You always think European hockey is going to be more wide open and with more scoring and that sort of stuff, but it's almost the opposite. There is less scoring….There was a lot more grabbing, holding and clutching than I expected. Because of the big ice, there's a lot of man-on-man play. In the playoffs, they were just draped all over me, and nothing got called. They let everything go. I remember forwards looking at me and not even looking at the play, with their stick between my legs."

–Dan Boyle, Tampa Bay Lightning defenseman,
on his season spent in Sweden

"I didn't really want to play, but in the back of your mind you always want to play, if that makes any sense. I don't think anybody retires without still wanting to play. I'll always want to play."

–Mark Messier, former NHL great, on his retirement

"He wouldn't listen. That's why I hit him."

–Maurice "Rocket" Richard, Montréal Canadiens
legend, on why he punched out referee
Cliff Thompson in the March 13, 1955, fight

"Americans could never, will never and cannot understand Shakespeare. They're far more fascinated with Cabbage Patch Dolls, the Hula Hoop and the local hockey team, which is largely made up of Canadians. That's the best joke of all."

–Marlon Brando, actor, while filming in Toronto in 1989

"I'm not planning a career change—not unless they need someone who constantly falls on the ice and is out of breath all the time."

–Scott Wolf, American actor, after playing
in a charity hockey game

"The hockey lockout of 1994–95 has been settled. They have stopped bickering…and can now get down to some serious bloodshed."

–O'Brien, host of Late Night with Conan O'Brien

"The place was always cold, and I got the feeling that the fans would have enjoyed baseball more if it had been played with a hockey puck."

–Andre Dawson, former Montréal Expos outfielder,
on playing baseball in front of Canadians

"The playoffs separate the men from the boys, and we found out we have a lot of boys in our dressing room."

> −*Neil Smith, New York Rangers general manager,*
> *after losing a series to the Washington Capitals*

"Excuse me, I'm going to go dive into the Stanley Cup."

> −*Mario Lemieux, former Pittsburgh Penguins great, after*
> *winning his second Stanley Cup against the Blackhawks in 1992*

"I led the league in hangovers. Fourteen years, every day."

> −*Gary Smith, NHL goaltender, who played*
> *on eight different teams in his 14-year career*

"He liked to present himself as this moody, aloof person, because then people would leave him alone. One time, a young boy got hit with a puck during a game. They brought him into the dressing room afterward, and Terry got his stick signed by all the players and gave it to the boy. Then he turned to me and said, 'If you tell the press about this, I'll kill you.' That's the way he was."

> −*Marcel Pronovost, NHL defenseman, on his former*
> *Detroit Red Wings teammate Terry Sawchuk*

"I start thinking about what I'm going to wear the next morning. I get the suit or jacket that I'm going to wear, and I hang it up in my bedroom. Before I go to bed, I put different ties with it. So, I'm thinking about that suit all week."

—Don Cherry, sportscaster and former NHL head coach, on picking out his infamous wardrobe for his Coach's Corner segment on CBC's Hockey Night in Canada

"Practice is cancelled tomorrow. No one else left to beat."

—Sign posted in the Canadian dressing room after a 3–2 World Cup Final victory over Finland

"American professional athletes are bilingual; they speak English and profanity."

—Gordie Howe, former Detroit Red Wings great

"I don't like my hockey sticks touching other sticks, and I don't like them crossing one another, and I kind of have them hidden in the corner. I put baby powder on the ends. I think it's essentially a matter of taking care of what takes care of you."

—Wayne Gretzky, former NHL great and current Phoenix Coyotes head coach, also a very superstitious hockey player!

"On the day of a game, I get up at 8:30 AM. I have my usual breakfast: orange juice, oatmeal, two slices of bread and a glass of milk. Then I head off to team training. When I get back, I always eat a hamburger steak and watch a show on TV. I have a 90-minute nap in the afternoon. Four hours before the game, I eat a plate of spaghetti. I arrive at the locker room at around 5:00 PM, and I put on my underwear. In the two and a half hours before warm-up, I chew 20 to 25 sticks of gum and drink lots of water. I tape up my three or four sticks for the game, and before every game, I jump in the dressing room spa for three or four minutes. Then I put on the rest of my equipment."

—Stéphane Lebeau (1968–), former NHL centre

"Fifty percent of the game is mental and the other 50 percent is being mental. I've got that part down, no problem."

—Basil McRae, former NHL left-winger

"It takes brains. It's not like a forward, where you can get away with scoring and not play defence. On defence, you have to be thinking."

—Chris Chelios, Detroit Red Wings defenseman

"I couldn't believe they'd beaten me on the play. I was sure the puck didn't quite cross the goal line. So I looked up at the big screen to watch the replay. Perhaps it would confirm I was right. While I was watching the replay, the referee dropped the puck and the play resumed. The Washington centreman won the draw and slipped the puck over to hard-shooting Mike Gartner. He stepped over the blue line and rifled a shot in my direction. But I didn't see the puck coming, because I was still watching the replay on the giant screen. That's when I heard my teammates screaming at me to wake up, and suddenly I knew I'd made a terrible faux pas."

—John Garrett, former NHL goaltender,
on letting in his worst goal ever

Chapter Four

International Flavour

Canadian Apology to Americans

I'm sorry we beat you in Olympic hockey. In our defence, I guess our excuse would be that our team was much, much, much, much better than yours. By way of apology, please accept all of our Canadian NHL teams, which, one by one, are going out of business and moving to your fine country.

–This Hour Has 22 Minutes

Q: How does Mats Sundin change a light bulb?

A: He holds it in the air, and the world revolves around him.

American Fans

New Jersey Devils goalie Martin Brodeur set the NHL mark for most wins by a goalie. This was such a historic moment in hockey, sports networks almost cut away from bass fishing to cover it.

Good Neighbours

Three Canadians and three Americans are travelling to a hockey game. The three Americans each buy tickets then watch as the three Canadians buy only one.

"How are the three of them going to travel on only one ticket?" asks an American.

"Watch and you'll see," says a Canadian.

They all board the train. The Americans take their respective seats, but all three Canadians cram into a bathroom and close the door behind them.

Shortly after the train has departed, the conductor comes around collecting tickets. He knocks on the bathroom door and says, "Ticket, please!" The door opens a crack, a single arm emerges with a ticket in hand. The conductor takes it and moves on. The Americans see this and agree that it is quite a clever idea.

After the game, they decide to copy the Canadians on the return trip and save some money. When they get to the station, they buy a single ticket for the return trip. To their astonishment, the Canadians don't buy any tickets at all.

"How are you going to travel without a ticket?" asks one perplexed American.

"Watch and you'll see," replies a Canadian.

When they board the train, the three Americans cram into a bathroom, and the three Canadians cram into another bathroom nearby.

Once the train leaves the station, one of the Canadians comes out and walks over to the bathroom where the Americans are hiding, knocks on the door and says, "Ticket, please!"

Middle East Peace?

A Canadian hockey fan, an American fan and a Swedish fan were visiting Saudi Arabia, and decided to share a smuggled crate of alcohol. All of a sudden, Saudi police rushed in and arrested them. The mere possession of alcohol is a severe offence in Saudi Arabia, so for the terrible crime of actually being caught consuming the alcohol, they were sentenced to death! However, after many months and with the help of very good lawyers, they were able to successfully appeal their sentence down to life imprisonment. By a stroke of luck, the day their trial finished was a Saudi national holiday, and the extremely benevolent Sheikh decided they could be released after receiving just 20 lashes of the whip each. As they were preparing for their punishment, the Sheikh suddenly said:

"It's my first wife's birthday today, and she has asked me to allow each of you one wish before your whipping."

The Swede fan was first in line (he had drunk the least), so he thought about this for a while and then said: "Please tie a pillow to my back."

This was done, but the pillow only lasted 10 lashes before the whip went through. The Swede fan had to be carried away bleeding and crying with pain when the punishment was done.

The American fan was next up (he'd almost finished half a can), and, after watching the scene, said: "All right! Please fix two pillows on my back." But even the two pillows could only take 15 lashes before the whip went through, sending the American fan crying.

The Canadian fan was the last one up (he had finished off the crate), but before he could say anything, the Sheikh turned to him and said: "You support the greatest team in the world, your country has the best and most loyal hockey fans in the world. For this, you may have two wishes!"

"Thanks, your most Royal highness," the Canadian replies. "In recognition of your kindness, my first wish is that you give me not 20 but 100 lashes."

"Not only are you an honourable, handsome and powerful man, you are also very brave," the Sheikh says with an admiring look on his face. "If 100 lashes is what you desire, then so be it. And your second wish? What is it to be?" the Sheikh asks.

"Tie the American fan to my back, so he can get his ass whooped again."

U.S. and Canada were playing a game of hockey against each other. About two-thirds of the way through the second period, a train passed the arena and blew its horn. The U.S. thought it was the end of the period and left the ice.

Q: How do you get European skaters into the corners?

A: Start a fight at centre ice!

Bimbo exam for Americans applying to become hockey fans:

1. Spell "puck."
2. What colour is the "blue line."
3. The goalie guards/defends what?
4. What colour jerseys do the Red Wings wear?
5. True or False: The Stanley Cup is an athletic supporter used by hockey players.
6. True or False: Uwe Krupp is not an illness that your little brother came down with last winter.
7. Pronounce "Yzerman."
8. True or False: The "C" on a player's jersey means "Come and Jump Me After the Game, baby."
9. True or False: The "A" on a player's jersey means "Available for Meaningless One-night Stands at Your Convenience."
10. True or False: That blond teenager who pals around with Sergei Federov is really his niece!

Movie Language

After arriving in America (from his native Czechoslovakia), Los Angeles Kings right-winger Zigmund Palffy did his best to learn to speak some English. His method? Watching Chris Farley movies and trashy talk shows.

"Did you hear about the American hockey fan who attended all the Montréal Canadiens home games?"

"No, what about him?"

"He thought the letters CH at centre ice stood for "Centre Hice.""

America and Hockey

America = More money for less talent. Buy from the Canadians.

Canadians and Hockey

Canada has more talent for less money. In Canada, the worst players get sold to the United States. Unless, of course, you're the Edmonton Oilers. Then you trade the good players away in a bad deal that ends up destroying the team.

The Iraqi Hockey Player

Toronto coach Pat Quinn sends scouts out around the world looking for a new centre who will hopefully help win the Stanley Cup for Toronto. One of his scouts informs him of a young Iraqi centre whom he thinks will turn out to be a true superstar. So, Pat flies to Iraq to watch him play, is suitably impressed and arranges for him to come over to the NHL.

Two weeks later, Toronto is down 4–0 at home against Montreal, with only eight minutes left. Pat gives the young Iraqi centre the nod to go on, and he puts him on in place of Sundin. The lad is a sensation, scores five goals in eight minutes and wins the game for Toronto. The fans are delighted, the players and coaches are delighted and the media love the new star. When he comes off the ice, he phones his Mum to tell her about his first day in the NHL.

"Hi, Mum, guess what?" he says. "I played for eight minutes today, we were down 4–0 but I scored five goals and we won. Everybody loves me. The fans, the players and the media, they all love me."

"Great," says his Mum, "let me tell you about my day. Your father got shot in the street, your sister and I were raped and beaten and your brother has joined a gang of looters, while you were having a great time."

The young lad is naturally very upset. "What can I say, Mum, I'm so sorry."

"Sorry!" says his Mum, "It's your damned fault that we moved to Toronto in the first place!"

Q: What's the difference between Bigfoot and a
      good American hockey players?

A: Bigfoot has actually been spotted.

An Italian was visiting Montréal, Canada. He
wanted to see a hockey game and noticed a man
carrying hockey stick.

"How do I get to the Montréal Forum?" the
Italian asked.

"Practice," said the smart Montréaler.

Cross-border Love

Two Americans boarded an American Airlines
flight out of Salt Lake after the gold-medal hockey
game. One sat in the window seat, and the other sat
in the middle seat. Just before take-off, a Canadian
got on and took the aisle seat. After take-off, the
Canadian kicked his shoes off, wiggled his toes and
was settling in, when the American in the window
seat said, "I think I'll get up and get a beer."

"No problem," said the Canadian, "I'll get it for you."

While he was gone, one of the Americans picked up
the Canadian's shoe and spat in it. When he returned
with the beer, the other American said, "That looks
good; I think I'll have one, too." Again, the Canadian
obligingly went to fetch it, and, while he was gone,
the other American picked up the other shoe and spat

in it. When the Canadian returned to his seat, they all sat back and enjoyed the flight. As the plane was landing, the Canadian slipped his feet into his shoes and knew immediately what had happened.

"Why does it have to be this way?" he asked. "How long must this go on? This fighting between our nations, this hatred, this animosity? This spitting in shoes and pissing in beers?"

The Bulgarian women's hockey team lost to Croatia by a whopping 82–0. If we're reading that right, they must have been playing the entire country of Croatia.

Q: How do Russians celebrate a Stanley Cup victory?

A: They go into town and get smashed.

Lunch

A Canadian hockey fan and a British hockey fan were camped outside the Bruins arena waiting for the hockey players to come out. The Brit pulled out his packed lunch. The Canadian asked, "What have you got?"

"Tongue sandwiches," replied the Brit.

"Yuck, I couldn't eat something that had come out of an animal's mouth," said the Canadian.

"Well what have you got then?" asked the Brit.

"Egg sandwiches."

A Russian hockey player commenting on an American sport in Canada:

In 1995, Russian centre Alexei Zhamnov saw his first (minor league) baseball game (in Winnipeg, Manitoba) and was completely underwhelmed. Midway through, he incredulously asked: "Do they shower after this?"

What you call a pro hockey player...

According to a report on *60 Minutes*, three members of the Canadian hockey team are being investigated for illegal steroid use. You know what you call a pro hockey player who doesn't take steroids?

An American player!

The United States squeaked out a tight 4–2 victory over Latvia at the ice hockey world championships. The game was closer than many expected, because the Americans were the only ones that could afford skates.

The U.S. Women's Hockey team beat Canada to win its second consecutive World Hockey Championship title. In related news, it's been a very, very slow day in the world of sports.

Pardon??

The Pittsburgh Penguins and Calgary Flames are in Pittsburgh playing a close game that is tied 1–1 late in the third period.

Just before a face-off, Jarome Iginla lines up next to Sidney Crosby and says, "Hey Crosby, you're a Canadian and playing hockey in America, right?"

Crosby swells out his chest and says, "Damn right I am and proud of it."

Iginla smiles and quips, " Then what are you in the bathroom?"

Crosby looks at Iginla and, appearing confused, asks, "What?"

To which Iginla laughs and responds, "European."

New Puck

The NHL had been testing a new type of puck and had passed it around various NHL teams, alphabetically, to get their opinion. Finally, they get around to Montréal, and the NHL official arrives at the Bell Centre and meets Bob Gainey.

"Here you go, sir, this is the Koivu puck...oops! I mean here's the new puck. Let us know what you think of it."

Gainey frowns and suspiciously asks, "Say, why'd you call it the Koivu puck?"

The official looks embarrassed and says, "Well, it's what the other teams have christened it..."

"Why?"

"It's unstable, doesn't handle being hit very well, isn't much good on the ice and won't be appearing in the playoffs."

Young Russian

The General Manager sat down with the young Russian hockey player and made him an offer.

"Okay" he said, "I'll give you $40,000 this year and twice as much in a year's time. What do you say?"

The young hockey player thought about it for a while. Finally, he said, "Sounds good. I'll be back in a year!"

Breaking News

The Canadians are finally going to help America with the War on Terrorism.

They pledged two of their biggest battleships, 600 ground troops and six fighter jets. With the exchange rate being what it is, the Americans ended up with two hockey players, one canoe and a flying squirrel.

Chapter Five

One-liners

Hockey players have been complaining about violence for years. It's just that without any teeth, no one can understand them.

Q: What is hockey?
A: A game with 12 players, two linesmen and 20,000 referees.

Q: Why is hockey like fresh milk?
A: It strengthens the calves.

Q: What do the Los Angeles Kings and the Titanic have in common?
A: They both look good until they hit the ice!

The dentist complimented the goalie on his nice, even teeth…one, three, seven, nine and eleven were missing.

I think hockey is a great game. Of course, I have a son who's a dentist.

Hockey was once a rich man's sport, but now it has millions of poor players.

Women's Hockey

Women's hockey is a really rough sport, especially on the goalies. They have to go through three periods with only two pads!

Q: Why is Cinderella such a crappy hockey player?
A: Because she had a pumpkin for a coach.

Q: What do you get if Wiarton Willie sees a Toronto Maple Leaf?
A: Six more weeks of bad hockey!

Q: What's the difference between a plane full of business travellers and a plane full of Montréal Canadiens fans?

A: When the engines on the plane full of business travellers stop, so does the whining sound.

Q: When dogs go to a hockey game, what do they like to do?

A: Chase the Zam'bone'y.

Q: What's the difference between a hockey mom and a hockey puck?

A: 20 IQ points.

Q: Why did the Tampa Bay Lightning try to sign Kurt Cobain?

A: They heard he was a killer on the faceoffs.

Bumper Sticker:
Be kind to animals.

Hug a hockey player.

I've created an invention that will revolutionize hockey and make it the wildest game on Earth. It's a clear Lucite puck!

Hockey is definitely too tough. I mean, what other sport has a coroner?

Hockey is becoming more violent. Last night's game looked like the Hell's Angels on Ice!

Reporter to hockey player: "Did you ever break your nose?" Player: "No, but 11 other players did!"

The RCMP is cracking down on speeders heading into Vancouver. For the first offence, they give you two Vancouver Canucks tickets. If you are stopped a second time, they make you use them.

Does anyone know if Poland found its recipe for making ice? I was hoping to see them ice a hockey team at the next Olympics.

The last time the Chicago Blackhawks won a Stanley Cup, most Hawks fans were in diapers. The next time the Hawks win a cup, some of these same fans will once again be in diapers.

Q: How did the blonde break her leg playing hockey for the Toronto Maple Leafs?

A: She fell out of the tree.

A toddler with eight limbs had successful surgery to remove four of those limbs. And thus the NHL lost the prospect of the greatest hockey goalie of all time.

Q: How do you know a leper is playing ice hockey?

A: There's a 'faceoff' in the corner.

Q: What's the difference between a hockey game and a prizefight?

A: In a hockey game, the fights are real.

The Boston Bruins are on the crest of a slump.

Q: Why do all the Penguins fans carry white towels?

A: They use them for crying into every time they lose to the Red Wings.

Football players have cheerleaders, but hockey players take them home.

Q: How many Lindroses does it take to change a light bulb?

A: Not even Eric knows, because his lights are always out.

Q: Why doesn't Hamilton have an NHL team?

A: Because then Toronto would want one....

The other day was "Take Your Daughter to Work" day. The Columbus Blue Jackets had a fun time playing a little scrimmage against their daughters. Unfortunately they lost 15–3.

Q: How can the Canadian men's Olympic ice
     hockey team hope to win?

A: Play like the Canadian women.

"You're so involved with hockey," whined the
wife, "that you can't even remember the day we
were married." "That's what you think!" countered
the husband. "It was the same day I scored a hat trick."

Q: What do the Texas Rangers and the Dallas Stars
     have in common?

A: Neither knows how to play hockey.

Q: Why was it so hot at Carolina Hurricanes games?

A: Because there was not a fan in the place.

Q: What happens to a hockey player when he
     becomes blind?

A: He becomes a referee!

Q: What do you call a North Americanized Asian hockey player?

A: Disoriented.

Q: Did you hear? New Jersey is building a new arena but is keeping its location hidden from the public.

A: Yeah, they're afraid the Devils will find out where it is and try to play there.

Q: What did the Inuit hockey player get from sitting on the ice too long?

A: Polaroids.

The head coach of the Anaheim Ducks asked one of his forwards, "Is your bad play due to ignorance or apathy?" The player replied, "I don't know, and I don't care!"

The Boston Bruins were so bad the coach had to prepare the team for the crowd noise they would hear during the season. He ran practices with a laugh track.

Hockey Marriage

One man to another, "My wife thinks I put hockey before marriage, even though we just celebrated our third season together."

Change

Tom said to his friend, "My sister has taken up hockey."

"Oh yeah? Does she like it?" asked the friend.

"Yeah, she's really good at it. In fact, she's so good, she's now my brother."

Bumper Sticker:

Hockey Players Do It on Thin Ice

Hockey Workout:

Hockey is a game in which a handful of men skate around for two hours watched by people who could really use the exercise.

Q: Why do the Atlanta Thrashers have yellow and purple jerseys?

A: So everyone is hung up on the ugly jerseys and no one notices that they suck!

An Ottawa Senators fan is a guy who'll yell at the forward all game for not spotting an open winger, then head for the parking lot and not be able to find his own car.

Q: Why did the Florida Panthers change their name to the Possums?

A: Because they play dead at home and get killed on the road.

Saturday Domestic Scene

Wife: "Hockey, hockey, hockey! That's all you ever think about! If you said you were going to stay at home one Sunday afternoon to help with the housework, I think I'd drop dead from shock!"

Husband: "It's no good trying to bribe me, dear."

Hockey player: That ointment the doctor gave me to rub on my knee really makes my hands smart.

Second player: Then, why don't you rub some into your head?

Q.   What do you call 30 millionaires around a TV watching the Stanley Cup playoffs?

A.   The New York Rangers.

Q.   How do you keep the Vancouver Canucks out of your yard?

A.   Put up a goal net.

Q.   What do you call a Buffalo Sabre with a Stanley Cup ring?

A.   A thief.

Q.   How many St. Louis Blues does it take to win a Stanley Cup?

A.   Nobody knows, and we may never find out.

Bumper Sticker:

Hockey Players Have Bigger Cups

The New York Islanders have a new coach from North Korea: Win Sum Soon.

Q: What's the difference between the Hawks and the Habs?

A: The Habs have a colour photo of their last Stanley Cup win.

Q: How many Montréal Canadiens fans does it take to screw in a light bulb?

A: One guy to screw in the light bulb, and three more to stand around smoking cigarettes and talking about how good the old light bulb was.

Q: Why doesn't Jesus play hockey?

A: Because he's scared to get nailed to the boards.

You hear about the guy from Calgary that left three booklets of season tickets for the Flames on his dash in an unlocked car at the mall?

When he came back there were eight booklets!

The Detroit Red Wings are back in the Stanley Cup Finals. When asked what they thought of being in the Super Bowl of hockey, all of Detroit responded, "What's the Super Bowl?"

Q: Why can't the Montréal Canadiens surf the World Wide Web?

A: Because they can't put three W's together!

Q: What do you call a Ottawa Senators player with half a brain?

A: Gifted!

Newspaper headline: "Hurricanes Get Blown Out."

Q: How do Islanders players' brain cells die?

A: Alone.

Q: Why do Edmonton Oilers hockey players write TGIF on their skates?

A: Toes Go In First.

Q: What happens when a Ottawa Senators player gets Alzheimer's disease?

A: His IQ goes up!

Q: Why did the Calgary Flames player scale the glass partition?

A: To see what was on the other side.

Q: What do you call 10 New York Rangers players standing ear to ear?

A: A wind tunnel.

Q: What did the Canadiens player say to the buxom waitress?

A: "'Debbie'...that's cute. What did you name the other one?"

Q: What does an Atlanta Thrashers player say when you blow in his ear?

A: Thanks for the refill!

Q: What is it called when a Leafs player blows in Senators player's ear?

A: Data transfer.

Q: What do you call a fly buzzing inside a Florida Panthers player's head?

A: A Space Invader.

Q: What's a Tampa Bay Lightning player's favourite rock group?

A: Air Supply.

Q: What do you see when you look into a Buffalo Sabres player's eyes?

A: The back of his head.

Q: Why do New Jersey Devils players drive VWs?

A: Because they can't spell PORSCHE!

Q: How do you make a Avalanche player laugh on Monday morning?

A: Tell them a joke on Friday night!

Q: How did the Kings player break his leg raking leaves?

A: He fell out of the tree.

Hockey and beer, the most wonderful of combinations. Sometimes the drunken crowd is more fun to watch than the game. In fact, some crowds get so rowdy, you'd swear the boards surrounding the rink weren't designed to stop the puck from hitting fans but to stop the fans from hitting players and refs!

Q: Why did the Canucks player try to steal a police car?

A: He saw "911" and thought it was a Porsche.

Q: What do you call a Ducks player in an institution of higher learning?

A: A visitor.

Q. Mikhail Grabovski and Jeff Finger went off a cliff in the bus. Why was everyone mad?

A. The bus could have seated the entire team.

A little known fact: the first testicular guard "cup" was used in hockey in 1874, but the first helmet wasn't used until 1974. In other words, it took 100 years for players to realize that their brains were also important!

Q: How many Edmonton Oilers will it take to win another Stanley Cup?

A: Nobody knows, and we may never find out. (It used to be just ONE, but they got rid of him.)

Yo Mama!

☛ Yo mama's so dumb, she drowned during the wave at the hockey arena.

☛ Yo mama is like a hockey player. She doesn't change her pad for three periods.

☛ Yo mama's so stupid, she tripped over the red line on a hockey rink.

☛ Your mama is so stupid, she took a rake to the Leafs game.

☛ Yo mama's so skinny, she used a needle for a hockey stick.

☛ Yo mama is like a hockey player. Everybody gets a shot.

Q: What did the hockey goalie say to his team-mate?

A: Let's get the "puck" out of here!

Q: Did you hear how the blonde hockey team
     drowned?

A: Spring training.

Why doesn't the fattest man in the world become
a hockey goalie?

Q: What is the difference between a Pittsburgh
     Penguins player with his hands up and a
     Detroit Red Wings player with his hands up?

A: A Penguins player will be holding a trophy. A Red
     Wings player will be surrendering.

Five guys at a hockey game:

Souvenirs: $150

Tickets: $250

Hotel and Beer: $500

Wives at home: PRICELE$$!

Bumper Sticker:
Hockey Without Nets is Figure Skating

Hockey players aren't always big, but somehow their bodies are always large enough to hold all the black and blue marks they get in a game.

Our home team wasn't doing well. During a typically horrible game, none of the players had even taken a shot on goal. Finally, one got the puck, and a voice from the stands yelled, "Shoot it! The wind's with you!"

When I was a kid, I thought that hockey players were sent to the penalty box to sit until their fathers came home from work. Come to think of it, that isn't such a bad idea.

Q: Why are referees' cell phones the best?

A: They take two minutes for charging.

Chapter Six

Anecdotes and Strangely True Tales

Most people know Maurice Richard as an intense and serious hockey player. His eyes pierced the soul of any goaltender he was breaking in on. But few people knew that he was quite the practical joker. Taking every chance he got, Richard would put soap or shaving cream in his teammates' shoes. His favourite joke was setting a guy's newspaper on fire while he was reading it.

Actual rules to end a hockey game in 19th-century Kingston:

When one team scores three goals;

When the men have to return to barracks;

When a player falls through the ice and is in danger of drowning.

Careful What You Wish For!

One day early in the 1975–76 season, after years of glory with the Boston Bruins, Phil Esposito was called in to meet with legendary Bruins coach Don Cherry. Cherry reluctantly told Esposito that he was being traded to another team.

"Okay," Esposito replied, "but if you say New York [Rangers], I'm going to jump out that window."

Cherry's reply?

"Bobby," he said, turning to an assistant, "open the window."

KGB

While visiting Moscow to play the Russians in the historic Summit Series in 1972, the Canadian hockey team was assigned a room in an elegant hotel, which they suspected had been bugged.

"We searched the room for microphones," Phil Esposito recalled. "In the centre of the room, we found a funny-looking, round piece of metal embedded in the floor under the rug. We figured we had found the bug. We dug it out of the floor and heard acrash beneath us. We had released the anchor to the chandelier in the ceiling below."

Copy Edit! Copy Edit! Copy Edit!

In May 2002, Ontario Hockey League MVP Brad Boyes (a first-round draft pick of the Toronto Maple

Leafs) and Cory Pecker (the league's top average player) led the Erie Otters to a victory in the Memorial Cup. Their triumph spawned this unfortunate headline: "Boyes, Pecker lift series lead to 3–0."

Only Amputation Used For Charity

Blues defenseman Paul Cavallini lost the tip of his finger when struck by a slapshot off the stick of Chicago's Doug Wilson in 1990. He later commented to the press that he had to "reach down into his glove to get the finger out." A local radio announcer for station KSHE gained possession of the severed digit after it was stolen by a pathology department hospital clerk following Cavallini's treatment. The radio announcer auctioned off the finger for a charity organization, despite Cavallini's shocked protestations.

Where Do the Hats Go?

During the 2008–2009 season, there were 69 hat tricks in total. As most people know, the tradition goes that when a hat trick is scored, people throw their hats out onto the ice in celebration. This means that 69 times during the season, hundreds of fans left the hockey arena without their head gear. Because the tradition of throwing your hat onto the ice began in the 1970s, hundreds of thousands of hats must have been collected over the years. So where do all these hats end up?

For years, fans have seen arena workers shovelling the hats into large plastic bins and carting them out of the arena. But what happens to them? The most obvious possibility is that workers simply throw them out. And, in fact, many are thrown away.

But the Director of Media Relations for the Carolina Hurricanes, Mike Sundheim, said in an interview with Greg Wyshynski of Yahoo Sports that a portion of the hats that are in decent shape are actually given to the players. Once the hats are collected, they are presented after the game to the player who scored the trick, and he decides if he wants to keep any as a memento of his accomplishment.

Alexander Ovechkin, who scored four hat tricks during the 2008–2009 season, is one player who likes to keep some of the hats, according to Nate Ewell of the Capitals. "Ovie has asked before where the hats were, and he's grabbed a hat or two. He even grabbed a red Caps hat at one point."

Some teams also donate hats that are not dirty or torn apart to charities. So if you ever see a homeless person in a hockey hat, maybe that's where it came from. (And if you threw your hat onto the ice, it might be a hat you recognize!)

Perhaps the most novel idea of what to do with the hats comes from the Columbus Blue Jackets. They displayed all the hat-trick hats collected since Geoff Sanderson scored the first one on February 10, 2001, in a giant transparent bin for all the fans to see.

Freudian Slip

During a Vancouver Canucks game one night, CKNW colour commentator Tom Larscheid made a memorable broadcasting blooper. "I just came back from the Canucks' dressing room," he reported, "and Pavel's groin has never felt better."

"Oh that was a great hand job by Skudra!" Larscheid exclaimed on another occasion. "He really helped out Ohlund with that one!"

Ahh, Come On, Ref!

Randy Pierce of the Colorado Rockies was so thrilled with his goal at 19:27 of the third period in their franchise's first win over the New York Islanders in 1979 that he picked the puck up off the ice after the goaltender tried to return it to the linesman for the face-off. Pierce kissed the puck and was given a two-minute penalty for delay of game.

Bloody Scream!

During a particularly rough hockey game one day, Camille Henry, one of the smallest players in the history of the National Hockey League, lost his temper and found himself brawling with one of the game's most feared enforcers, a rugged defenseman named Fernie Faman, who outweighed him by some 75 pounds.

As they grappled, gripped and grabbed, angling for advantage, pint-sized Henry suddenly shouted a warning to his enormous opponent: "Watch out, Fernie," he exclaimed, "or I'll bleed all over you!"

Only Team to Score Nine Goals in One Period of Play

The Sabres set a record with nine goals in one period in a 14–4 pounding of the Leafs in March 1981. Buffalo led 1–0 at the end of the first, but a nine-goal, record-setting onslaught on goalie Michel Larocque followed in the second.

Rookies!

Nashville Predators defenseman Bill Houlder once recalled facing Mario Lemieux (thought by many to have been the most talented offensive player in hockey history) as a rookie in 1987:

"Somehow, I got stuck out there against him, and he was coming down the ice one-on-one with me. I was trying to watch his chest, but I kept seeing his arms going back and forth, moving the puck down by my feet. I was thinking, 'That puck's got to be right down there.'"

Alas, Houlder then made a rookie mistake: "When I finally looked down, my feet were weaving so badly that I fell flat on my backside...."

Did Lemieux walk in on a breakaway and score? Not exactly. Luckily for Houlder, he had landed on the puck!

Lemieux, ever the gentleman, later apologized. "He said, 'Sorry about that, kid.' I said, 'That's all right. I don't think you'll have to worry about seeing me out here too much more tonight.'"

Poetic Justice

During a game against the Colorado Avalanche one night in Colorado, Chicago Blackhawks right winger Steve Sullivan was hit in the face by an errant puck. Adding insult to injury was an obnoxious fan in the stands who laughed at and mocked Sullivan for several minutes.

Some time later, Sullivan, having endured a dozen stitches and returned to the game, was amused to see Avalanche goaltender Patrick Roy accidentally clear the puck over the boards, giving the Blackhawks a two-minute power play for delay of game, while simultaneously doling out a dollop of poetic justice: the puck, incredibly, hit the obnoxious fan in the face, giving him a bloody nose. Sullivan, not missing his chance, skated over to the fan, pointed to his forehead and laughed right back at him.

Oops!

In the final minute of a close NHL hockey game between the Buffalo Sabres and the Toronto Maple Leafs in February 2004, Toronto pulled goalie Trevor Kidd and sent out an extra attacker to try to tie the game. Leafs centre Robert Reichel, attempting a pass

from behind the Buffalo net after Sabres goalie Mika
Noronen had made a save, sent the puck the length
of the ice into his own net with 43 seconds remaining.

Although the goal was initially credited to Dmitri
Kalinin, an official scoring change gave the goal to
Noronen, who became the first Sabres goalie in history to score in an NHL game. When Noronen heard
the news (in the Buffalo dressing room 10 minutes
after the game) he teased teammate Eric Boulton
about having more goals than him. "It's pretty funny,
actually," Noronen remarked. "I can say I'm one of
the leading defence scorers on the team now!"

Initiation

"I was once a rookie player," the legendary hockey
reporter Red Fisher once recalled, "and I had to be
initiated by the Montréal Canadiens on the train.
The Rocket [Maurice Richard] came to me one day,
and he said, 'We were looking for you on the train
last week.' I said, 'Rock, I'm flying now, but I've got
to tell you, I know what you have got in mind, and
the first person who comes toward me is gonna get
punched right in the jaw.' Big mistake.

"The Rock organized this thing, and, instead of
doing it on the train, they decided for the first and
last time, they would do it at the Forum, and he
arranged the whole bit. He had Dickie Moore call me
at home and say, 'There's a big story breaking at the
Forum tomorrow. Are you coming to the Forum?'
And I said, 'No, it's my day off.' And he said, 'You
better come.' And I said, 'No, I'm not. It's the dead of

winter and I'm not coming down to the Forum.'
Then he hung up the phone, and I thought about it,
and I said, 'I can't miss a big story, right...?'

"So I go down there.... It took 18 of the cowards
to get me, but they did a king-size job, with the
Rocket walking in after they had hog-tied me to
a table outside the main dressing room, and he was
wearing the white cap and the white jacket and
a white mask and the shaver..."

Fear of Flying

The public has an image of hockey players as fear-
less athletes who can meet any challenge placed before
them, but sometimes these towers of strength get
weak in the knees when it comes to sitting in an
airplane for a few hours. Most famous among those
players was Wayne Gretzky, the "Great One" himself.

Gretzky was one of the coolest-headed players in
the league, able to effortlessly skate down the ice and
make incredible plays without seeming to break
a sweat. But put the greatest player in hockey history
on a plane, and you would see a completely different
person. Even before takeoff, sweat would pour down
his face, his hands would tremble and, not butter-
flies but bulls would be tearing around in his stomach.
Even the slightest bit of turbulence would put the
Great One into a panic. Things got so bad for Gretzky
that he even sought out professional help for his
phobia because, with all the public appearances he
had to make beyond the travel time for games, it was
starting to affect his life.

"It got better when I asked to see the cockpit and, on some flights, I was allowed to sit there for a time, watch how they were flying the plane, even if I never understood it, and it helped me relax a little," said Gretzky.

Confused

St. Louis Blues defenseman Noel Picard would rather forget one particular game against the Boston Bruins, but it is just too embarrassing to let pass. During the course of the game, after an extra-long shift, Picard was extremely tired and needed to get to the bench. But, in his exhaustion, he sat down on the opposing team's bench. The Bruins players could barely keep themselves from falling off the bench with laughter. On the other side of the rink, Blues coach Scotty Bowman was the only one not laughing. When he tried to skate back to his bench, the referee caught him and assessed the Blues a penalty for having too many men on the ice. Hey Noel, that's why teams have different jerseys!

True Story

Bee Swarm disrupts Red Wings Cup celebration: Columbus Blue Jackets deny involvement!

Detroit, MI: A swarm of angry bees descended upon revellers celebrating the Detroit Red Wings Stanley Cup Hockey Championship this weekend. The attack occurred shortly after a float honouring

Red Wings great, Paul Coffey, passed through the parade route. "I don't know where they came from" said Jasper Milk. "They were everywhere. They attacked us like a huge swarm of...of...well, I guess, like a huge swarm of bees." No injuries were reported, although several bees were found drowned in leftover cups of Miller Lite, which lined the parade route.

More Cherry

Ever hear of an NHL coach calling a time-out in a game to sign autographs? Don Cherry did it the night he coached the woeful Colorado Rockies to an upset victory over his former team, the Boston Bruins. It was December 2, 1979, and Cherry was itching for a win when he brought his Rockies into the Boston Garden for the first time since he was dismissed as the Bruins' coach in the off-season.

The Boston fans were quick to show Cherry he was missed and loved, rising to give him a standing ovation when he took his place behind the visiting team's bench. As usual, the Rockies got off to a sluggish start and fell behind 2–0. Then someone said, "Come on, guys, let's dig in and win this for Grapes." And they did, squeezing out a 5–3 victory, with the last shot hitting the empty Boston net. The most talked-about moment in the game came during the third period, when Cherry called a time-out. His players gathered at the bench, but he discussed no strategy, offered no words of encouragement. To their amazement, and to the delight of everyone in the building, he turned his back on them and started signing autographs.

"It was just somethin' that happened," he said later. "I didn't plan it. I wasn't tryin' to twist the knife in or nothin'. I was just tryin' to give my defensemen a rest. Then people started askin' me for my autograph, so I signed some things. You can bet my bosses in Colorado weren't too happy about that."

True Story

Los Angeles Kings forward Luc Robitaille was drilled into the net during a scramble in a Vancouver Canucks-Kings game. Acting out of instinct, he quickly turned and drilled the first player he saw with a cross-check. Unfortunately, it was teammate Dave Taylor. As Taylor groggily rose to his feet, seeking revenge, Robitaille, in a state of panic, pointed to nearby Vancouver defenseman Doug Lidster. "It was him," Robitaille told Taylor, who immediately lunged at Lidster. Robitaille waited nearly two years before revealing what had really happened.

Hockey Has Changed

The legendary Toronto Maple Leafs general manager Conn Smythe was well known for his fiery personality and stubborn work ethic that often put him at odds with players and managers around the league. But one general manager in particular raised Smythe's heart rate more than any other.

Conn Smythe and Boston Bruins general manager Art Ross never liked each other. The Leafs and Bruins were bitter rivals, and each manager did whatever it took to get under the other's skin. From his playing days in the NHL, Ross was used to players' underhanded tactics and mental games, but, as good as Ross could dish it out, Smythe was equally adept at those underhanded tactics. For no better reason than to inflame the passions of the Bruins faithful and to get under Ross's skin, Smythe took out a full-page ad in a Boston newspaper declaring, "Attention Hockey Fans! If you're tired of seeing the kind of hockey the Boston Bruins are playing, come to the Gardens (Maple Leaf Gardens) tonight and see a real hockey club, the Toronto Maple Leafs!" To say the least, Ross was not impressed.

As stubborn and cantankerous as Smythe was, Ross was every bit his equal. Ross had distinguished himself first as a player in the pre-NHL days and then as a referee and general manager for the Hamilton Tigers. When a team was placed in Boston, owner Charles Adams could think of no better person than Art Ross for the job of vice-president, general manager and head coach. But the new responsibilities of Ross's position did little to calm the fiery nerves of the former player. He began his habit of feuding with other general managers when he made New York Americans Red Dutton a target of his ire.

At an NHL board-of-governors meeting in 1936, Ross made Dutton his target for some reason only he knew. The other governors in attendance at the

meeting could see that Red Dutton was indeed turning red in the face the more Ross got under his skin.
As the tension began to build, James Norris, manager of the Detroit Red Wings decided to step in
before things got out of hand. Unfortunately for
Norris, the moment he stepped between the two,
Ross threw a punch at Dutton, and Norris's face got
in the way. Furious at the attempted sucker punch,
Dutton jumped Ross and proceeded to punch him
mercilessly, until Ross left the meeting with a broken nose, a fractured cheek and a few missing teeth.

Off With his Hair

Early in his career, Bobby Hull was known for
two things: his amazing offensive talent on the ice
and for his golden locks that flowed gracefully in the
air as he sped down the ice to score one of his many
goals. With his chiselled good looks and amazing
offensive talent, the "golden jet" was the poster boy
for the NHL. He was also extremely sensitive about
his hair, especially when it started to fall out. Unable
to come to terms with losing his hair, Hull became
the first player in National Hockey League history to
wear a toupee.

Of course, every player in the NHL knew Hull wore
a hairpiece, but none were foolish enough to mess
the golden one's new do. Known for his scoring
prowess, Hull was also not one to shy away from
a challenge, and he had 15-inch biceps to back him
up. The intimidation did not outweigh the sheer

curiosity of Steve Durbano, who played for the Birmingham Bulls of the now-defunct World Hockey Association. On April 14, 1978, during a playoff game versus Hull's Winnipeg Jets, Durbano decided to have a look under Hull's rug.

When a fight broke out in the corner of the rink and several players were distracted pulling players off each other, Durbano skated up behind Hull, who was preoccupied with another player, and proceeded to rip off the toupee, exposing Hull's bald head for everyone to see. Too embarrassed to pursue his hairpiece, Hull rushed to the dressing room. When he returned to action, he was wearing a helmet and several shades of red on his face.

Not that Kind of Bowl

It is traditional after a team wins the Stanley Cup for players to take turns drinking champagne from the bowl, but in the Cup's long history, many other substances have found their way into bowl that would make you think twice before ever letting it touch your lips.

The first horrifying story came after the Detroit Red Wings won the Stanley Cup in 1937. During the celebrations, after consuming copious amounts of alcohol, Red Wings forward Gord Pettinger mistook the legendary trophy for a bowl of the porcelain kind and promptly filled it with urine.

Many fans and players refer to the Stanley Cup as the Holy Grail of hockey and consider any defilement as a sacrilege that risks a curse being placed on the player or team. The New York Rangers were made firm believers in the curse after winning the 1940 Stanley Cup Championship.

Not only did the entire New York Rangers team use the Cup as their personal toilet, but Rangers president John Kilpatrick also burned the deed to the fully paid mortgage on Madison Square Garden in the bowl of the Cup. These two desecrations of the sacred Stanley Cup did not go unnoticed by the hockey gods. Legend goes that a curse was placed on the team. That curse would last 54 years, until the Stanley Cup once again graced the halls of Madison Square Garden.

Whether they're believers or not, most professional players will not leave anything to chance and dare not mess with the hockey gods. However, that is not the worst thing to have found its way into the Stanley Cup. The ultimate sacrilege came from an innocent child.

Just moments after winning the Stanley Cup in 1964, the Toronto Maple Leafs' Red Kelly was forced to leave the celebrations to catch a train to Ottawa to attend to more pressing matters as an honourable member of Parliament representing the liberal party and the good people of York West, Ottawa. Because of his extracurricular activities, Kelly never got a chance to have his photo taken with the Cup. So Leafs owner Harold Ballard, being the nice guy he is, had the Cup and a photographer sent to the Kelly household for a photo session.

The entire Kelly family gathered for the photo session in the living room, even Kelly's infant son. Thinking it would make a really cute picture Kelly placed his naked infant son in the bowl of the cup for the shot. The picture was a wonderful memory, but his son left behind some memories of his own.

"He did the whole load in the Cup. He did everything," said Kelly in a later interview. "That's why our family always laughs when we see players drinking champagne from the Cup."

Would you still take that drink?

Marital Bliss

Bobby Hull was known as one of the nicest of guys off the ice, sometimes holding up the team bus for hours just to sign autographs for his fans. Hull's superstar status gave him a certain notoriety among the opposite sex, and rumours about his fidelity to his first wife, Joanne, were rampant. To say the least, his relationship with his wife was not one of harmony.

As Ralph Mellanby reports in his book, *Walking With Legends*, after Hull had been partying the night before, his wife stood behind the glass at the Chicago Blackhawks pre-game warm-up giving him her best evil eye. Unable to bare the glare from his wife, Hull blasted a shot right at her head. With his powerful slapshot, which was often considered the hardest ever, he was lucky he didn't break the glass in the process.

"Maybe I should shoot at her," teammate Stan Mikita suggested. "I have a harder shot than you do."

"Be my guest," Hull replied.

The Satirical History of the Stanley Cup

The Stanley Cup is a $50 upside-down silver bowl awarded annually to the champions of the National Hockey League. It was named for Stanley of Stanley Tools, who crafted the cup while marooned in Montréal in a sea of French-speakers. Conspiracy theorists, however, maintain that it was named for Stanley Cuprick, for his years of service as a *Hockey Night in Canada* cameraman.

The Cup was first awarded in 1893 to the Montréal Eh? Eh? Eh? It became a tradition for the hockey players to etch all their names, along with the names of their lovers, inside little hearts on the side of the crystal. (Unfortunately, the 1895 Montréal Victorians captain Oscar Wilde etched "Oscar + Alfie" and got himself into some legal trouble.) The Cup was inadvertently smashed, when a member of the 1905 Ottawa Silver Seven drop-kicked it onto the frozen Rideau Canal. (As he explained to league authorities: "I didn't realize water froze in the cold.") Today, the NHL uses a replica of the Cup, and the names of players' lovers are kept on a CD, so they don't have to keep being re-etched every time the Cup gets smashed. (It also prevents conflicts, such as those that occurred numerous times, when the players handed names to the engraver, only to find afterward that some women were listed more than once).

The cup is presented on the ice to the captain of the NHL champions. The captain lifts it above his head and kisses it repeatedly, then skates around the arena to the cheers of thousands. The players pass the cup among themselves, each in turn hoisting and kissing it. They then take it to the locker room, where it is filled with champagne (though someone always spikes it with juice). And if you think all this kissing and cup-sharing is pretty gross, just consider that the Cup has several times been used as a urinal.

The Stanley Cup is kept at the Hockey Hall of Infamy in Toronto, Ontario. It can be viewed by the general public, except when it is stolen for brief periods to film beer commercials. It also tours hometowns of each of the winning team's players. When asked what it was going to do following the 2007 championship won by the Disney-owned Anaheim Waddling Wimps, the Cup declared: "I'm gonna go to Disneyland!"

True Story

It's not drunk driving in New Jersey if it involves a Zamboni.

A judge ruled that the four-ton, ice-rink grooming machines aren't motor vehicles because they aren't useable on highways and can't carry passengers.

Zamboni operator John Peragallo had been charged with drunk driving in 2005, after a fellow employee at the Mennen Sports Arena in Morristown told police the machine was speeding and nearly crashed into the boards.

Police said Peragallo's blood alcohol level was 0.12 percent. A level of 0.08 is considered legally drunk in New Jersey.

Peragallo appealed, and Superior Court Judge Joseph Falcone on Monday overturned his license revocation and penalties.

Chapter Seven

Religion

The Goaltender's Psalm
The puck is my shepherd;

I shall not ice.

It maketh me save in unnatural positions;

It leadeth me into leg splits;

It restoreth my fans' faith;

It leadeth me in the paths of odd-man rushes.

Yea, though I skate in the valley of the shadow of
the net,

I will fear no sniper;

For my stick is with me;

My facemask and pads, they comfort me;

I annointeth my body with sports cream;

My back-up tippeth over!

Surely coaches and trainers shall follow me

All the games of my life.

And I shall dwell in the Montréal Forum forever.

The Player's Psalm, by Loralyn Bemis

The coach is my shepherd;

I shall not get penalties.

He maketh me to do skating drills.

My captain leadeth me into games;

He restoreth my faith;

He leadeth me into the path of winning games for
the team's sake.

Yea, though I face the wrath of the coach,

I will fear no evil,

For my stick is with me.

My pads and my helmet, they comfort me;

They preparest game situations for me.

In the presence of my rivals

They annointest my body with sweat.

My water bottle runneth over.

Surely stats and games shall follow me

For all the days of my career,

And I will dwell on winning the Stanley Cup
forever.

Sinner?

A great hockey player was killed tragically, and,
arriving at heaven's gates, he came face to face with
the angel on duty.

"Is there any reason why you shouldn't be allowed
to enter the kingdom of heaven?" asked the angel.

"Well," said the hockey player, "there was one time when I cheated in the Stanley Cup playoffs."

"I see," said the angel, "tell me about it."

"Well," said the hockey player, "I was playing for the Montréal Canadiens against the Toronto Maple Leafs, and I used my skate to kick in a goal. The referee didn't see it, and it counted."

"And what was the final score?" asked the angel.

"That was the only goal," said the hockey player. "We won 1–0 and took the Cup back to Montréal."

"Well, that's not too serious. I think we can let you in," said the angel.

"Oh, *merveilleux*!" exclaimed the hockey player. "It's been on my mind for years. Thanks a lot, St. Peter."

"That's okay," said the angel, ushering the hockey player in. "And by the way, it's St. Peter's day off today. I'm St. Jean Baptiste."

Hell!

A passionate hockey fan died and went to hell. After a few days, the Devil came up to him and said, "What do you feel like doing today? You can have anything you like."

Thinking hell was not as bad as everyone had made it out to be, the hockey lover said, "Well, I can think of nothing better to do than play a game of hockey. Can we do that?"

"Certainly," said the Devil, and off they went to get changed for the game.

Coming out of the dressing room, he wore the best equipment he had ever seen: the sharpest skates, a golden stick. The ice was perfect. The hockey player took to the ice and prepared himself for the opening face-off. Nothing happened.

"Come on then," he said to the Devil, "drop the bloody puck."

"Ah, you see, that's the hell of it," said the Devil with a smile on his face. "We haven't got any pucks."

Pearly Gates

A man knocked on the pearly gates. His face was old, and his clothes were stained. He trembled and shook with fear as St. Peter spoke: "What have you done to gain admission here?"

"Sir, I've been a loyal Montréal Canadiens fan all my life," said the man.

The pearly gates suddenly swung open.

"Come in and choose your harp angel," St. Peter said. "You've had your share of hell."

Q: What do the Philadelphia Flyers and a preacher have in common?

A: They each make 20,000 people stand up and scream Jesus Christ!

Old Timers

Three old hockey fans are in a church one September Sunday, praying for their teams.

The first one asks, "Lord when will the Oilers win the Stanley Cup again?"

God replies, "In five years."

"But I'll be dead by then," says the man.

The second one asks, "Lord, when will the Flames win the Stanley Cup?"

The Lord answers, "In 10 years."

"But I'll be dead by then," says the man.

The third one asks, "Oh Lord when will the Leafs win the Stanley Cup again?"

God answers, "I'll be dead by then!"

The Leafs Have Won the Stanley Cup!

One day, Satan was out for a walk through hell, making sure things were running smoothly. When he got to the Lake of Fire, he saw a man sitting by the lake, relaxing in a lawn chair without sweating or looking uncomfortable at all. Perplexed, Satan approached the man and asked, "Young man, are you not hot or bothered by this heat?"

The man replied, "Oh no, not at all. I lived in downtown Ottawa, and this weather is just like a typical July day in the city."

Satan thought that this was not a good sign. So he rushed back to his office and turned up the heat in hell another 100 degrees. Satisfied with himself, he again returned to the Lake of Fire to check on the young man.

When he got there, the man was showing a few beads of sweat, but that was all. Again Satan asked the Ottawa native, "Are you hot and uncomfortable yet?"

The young man looked up and said, "No, the temperature is just like a hot August day in Ottawa. I'm coping with it just fine."

Satan decided that he had to do something drastic to make this man's stay in hell unpleasant. He went back to his office, turned the heat all the way down and then turned up the air conditioning. The temperature in hell quickly dropped well below zero. As he approached the Lake of Fire, he noticed that it was now frozen over. He also saw the young man jumping up and down wildly, waving his arms and yelling into the air.

"This looks promising!" thought Satan. Coming closer, he finally made out what the man was shouting: "The Leafs have won the Stanley Cup! The Leafs have won the Stanley Cup!"

That's My Boy!

Four women were having coffee and bragging about their children. The first woman says, "My son is a priest. When he walks into a room, everyone calls him Father."

The next woman tries to top her. "Really? My son married the princess of a small European country, and when he walks into the room, people call him Your Highness!"

The third woman chirps, "Well, my son is a cardinal of the church. Whenever he walks into a room, people call him Your Eminence!"

The fourth woman is just sitting there, sipping her coffee silently, and the other three look at her in a subtle way, as if to say "well...?"

She smiles and says, "Oh. My son is a very large and handsome hockey player. Whenever he walks into a room, women say, "Oh my god!"

The Voice of God

A drunk decides to go ice fishing, so he gathers his gear and goes walking around until he finds a big patch of ice. He heads to the centre of the ice and begins to saw a hole. Suddenly, a loud booming voice comes out of the sky. "You will find no fish under that ice."

The drunk looks around but sees no one. He starts sawing again. Once more, the voice speaks. "As I said before, there are no fish under the ice."

The drunk looks all around, high and low but can't see a single soul. He picks up the saw and tries one more time to finish.

Before he can even start cutting, the huge voice interrupts. "I have warned you three times now. There are no fish!"

The drunk is now flustered and somewhat scared, so he asks the voice, "How do you know there are no fish? Are you God trying to warn me?"

"No," the voice replies. "I am the manager of this hockey rink."

Bad Priest

A New York Rangers hockey fan was driving home from work and passes a local priest. He stops and offers him a lift. The priest thanks him kindly, and together they proceed to the church to drop the priest off.

On the way to the church, they pass a man walking his dog on the other side of the road; on closer inspection, it becomes clear that the man is wearing a New York Islanders jersey. Now the driver hates the Islanders and suddenly feels an uncontrollable urge to run his car into the man. He puts his foot down on the accelerator and tries to hit him, but, at the last minute, the Islanders fan jumps out of the way. The driver of the car thinks he'd heard a bang but realizes with relief that he's missed him.

The two men proceed to the church in silence, with the New York Rangers fan feeling more and more guilty for what he'd tried to do. When they pull to a stop, he says, "Look, Father, I'm really sorry about that incident back there. I don't know what came over me. Can you forgive me?"

The priest replies, "There's nothing to forgive you for. Everybody misses sometimes, and, anyway, I got him with the car door."

Fixed Game

St. Peter and Satan were having an argument one day about hockey. Satan proposed a game be played on neutral ice between a select team from the heavenly host and his own handpicked boys.

"Very well," said the gatekeeper of heaven. "But you realize, I hope, that we've got all the good players and the best coaches."

"I know, but that's all right," Satan replied unperturbed. "We've got all the referees."

Why?

The 2004 Stanley Cup Playoffs have just ended, and a Calgary Flames fan is walking home from the bar where he watched the game. He's about to cross the street, when he hears someone whisper, "Don't cross, you'll get hit by a car."

He looks around for the speaker and then sees a car come flying through the red light in just the spot he would have been if he had crossed the road.

"Who are you?" the fan asks.

"I'm your guardian angel," the voice answers. "I prevent bad things from happening to you."

"Wait a second. If you're my guardian angel, you've got some explaining to do," the fan replies.

"Ah, you want to know why I let Calgary lose. Well, you see…"

"No, actually, I was going to ask where you were when I became a Flames fan."

Goaltender Prayer

The goaltender threw a party after his team won the championship and, as a special honour, asked his coach to say grace.

Finishing up the prayer, the coach said, "We thank you, oh Lord, in the name of the Father, the Son and the goalie host."

Hockey Players versus Monks

A hockey team from Illinois played a match against a team from a visiting monastery. Just before the first period, the visiting team, all of whom were monks, knelt solemnly on the ice, put their hands together and indulged in five minutes of silent prayer. The monastery then proceeded to trounce their hosts 13–1. After the match, the Illinois captain said, "Well boys, we've been out-played before, but this is the first time we've ever been out-prayed."

IQ Test

Three men died and went to heaven, where St. Peter quizzed each one.

"What's your IQ?" St. Peter asked the first man, from Montréal.

"210."

"Maybe then we can discuss String Theory and the multiverse hypothesis some time." St. Peter then turned to the second man, from Toronto.

"What's your IQ?"

"178."

"Maybe we can talk about geopolitical issues some time." St. Peter then turned to the third man, from Edmonton. "What's your IQ?"

"40!" he said proudly.

"Hey, how about those Oilers?"

Crafty Nuns

Three guys were sitting behind three nuns at a hockey game. The men decided to antagonize the nuns to get them to move. So the first guy says to the others, loudly enough for the women to hear, "I think I want to move to Chicago; there are only 100 Catholics living there."

The second guy speaks up and says, "I want to move to Pittsburgh; there are only 50 Catholics living there."

The third guy speaks up and says, "I want to move to New York; there are only 25 Catholics living there."

One of the nuns turns around, looks the third guy in the eye and says calmly, "Why don't you go to hell? There aren't any Catholics there."

Fishing Pope

The Pope is marlin fishing one day, when he spots a distant boat that appears to be having some trouble hauling something out of the water. He quickly steers his cruiser toward the boat. As he gets nearer, he sees half a dozen fishermen. They are all wearing San Jose Sharks fan gear and are pulling a dishevelled, almost-drowned man dressed in Ducks gear onto the deck of the boat with a long rope. Knowing of the intense rivalry between San Jose and Anaheim, the Pope is suitably impressed. He exclaims:

"God bless you, my sons! That is a wonderful thing—saving a man from certain death, in spite of your differences! May heaven shine all its glory on all of you!"

With that, he sprinkles holy water on the boat, crosses himself, blesses the boat and speeds away.

The Sharks fans just look at each other, dumbfounded.

Says one, "What was that all about?"

Says another, "I have no idea."

Says another, "Listen, we gotta get going here. Stuff five more fish into this guy's jersey and we'll probably catch that shark on the next pass!"

Easter

Three Canadian blondes died and found themselves standing before St. Peter. He told them that before they could enter the kingdom, they had to tell him what Easter represented.

The first blonde said, "Easter is a holiday where we have a big feast, and we give thanks and eat turkey."

St. Peter said, "Noooooo," and he banished her to hell.

The second blonde said, "Easter is when we celebrate Jesus' birth and exchange gifts."

St. Peter said, "Noooooo," and he banished her to hell.

The third blonde said she knew what Easter was, and St. Peter said, "So, tell me."

She said, "Easter is a Christian holiday that coincides with the Jewish festival of Passover. Jesus was having Passover feast with his disciples when Judas betrayed him. The Romans arrested him, stuck him to a cross and eventually he died. Then they buried him in a tomb behind a very large boulder."

Astonished, St. Peter said, "Very good!"

Then the blonde continued, "Now, every year, the Jews roll away the boulder, and Jesus comes out. If he sees his shadow, we have six more weeks of hockey."

And St. Peter fainted.

Heavenly Golf

Moses, Jesus and Alexander Ovechkin were out playing golf one day. Moses pulled up to the tee and drove a long one. It landed in the fairway but rolled directly toward a water hazard. Quickly, Moses raised his club, the water parted and it rolled to the other side, safe and sound.

Next, Jesus strolled up to the tee and hit a nice long one directly toward the same water hazard. It landed directly in the centre of the pond and kind of hovered over the water. Jesus casually walked out onto the pond and chipped it up onto the green.

Ovechkin got up and sort of randomly whacked the ball. It headed out over the fence and into oncoming traffic on a nearby street. It bounced off a truck and hit a nearby tree. From there it bounced onto the roof of a nearby shack and rolled down into the gutter, down the downspout, out onto the fairway and right toward the same pond. On the way to the pond, it hit a stone and bounced out over the water and onto a lily pad where it rested quietly. Suddenly, a large bullfrog jumped up on the lily pad and took the ball into his mouth. Just then, an eagle swooped down and grabbed the frog and flew away. As they passes over the green, the frog squealed with fright and dropped the ball, which bounced right into the hole for a beautiful hole in one.

Moses turned to Jesus and said, "Does he think he is God, now?"

Chapter Eight

Lists and Other Oddities

Top 10 Signs You Have a Bad Goalie

10. Keeps telling the goal judge to "Get ready!"

9. Mask painted like Malibu Barbie.

8. On the net with his squeeze bottle is a box of Kentucky Fried Chicken.

7. Wearing Mr. Magoo–esque glasses over his mask.

6. You find him in a fetal position in the corner of the net.

5. Ice-level microphone keeps picking up sounds of him praying.

4. He's wearing a virtual reality mask.

3. Keeps using his big stick to tenderize meat.

2. Technique for stopping breakaways: fakes seizures.

1. Tries not to get hit by the puck.

Top 10 Signs There's a Rookie in the Dressing Room

10. The only guy in the room who can't grow a playoff beard.

9. He actually follows curfew.

8. He keeps asking, "Can I drive the Zamboni? Can I? Can I, please?"

7. Has Pro-Active in his locker.

6. He blushes every time he sees the cheerleaders.

5. Is scared of girls.

4. Can't buy beer for the team.

3. Playoff beard is more like playoff fuzz.

2. Growing up, he idolized Sidney Crosby.

1. Cries for his mom on road trips.

Ten Reasons to Date a Hockey Player

10. They always wear protection.

9. They have great hands.

8. They are used to scoring.

7. They have great stamina.

6. They find the opening and get it in.

5. They never miss the target.

4. They know how to use their wood.

3. They have long sticks.

2. They know when to play rough.

1. Baseball players only know how to hit balls.

Top 10 Reasons Not to Date a Hockey Player

10. They're always hugging each other.

9. They don't know how not to play rough.

8. Their sticks break.

7. They can't get wood.

6. They often miss the target.

5   They can't always find the opening.

4. They work in 45-second shifts.

3. They always want to do it on the ice.

2. When they make a nice move, they want to see the slow-motion replay.

1. Their protection doesn't always work.

Top 10 Hockey Pickup Lines

10. "So, this guy says he hates hockey players because they have no tact and are easily distracted. So I— Hey! Babe! Wanna do the nasty?"

9. "You heard right: I only take off this mask for two things."

8. "I may be toothless, sweaty and all black and blue, but I make a mean quiche Lorraine."

7. "Me take you eat."

6. "Would you like a Zamboni ride?"

5. "Tho...what'th your thighn?"

4. "C'mon baby, the iceman cometh...but never too soon."

3. "Well if I can't score, can I get an assist?"

2. "You know, less teeth means more tongue!"

1. "You want to check my stick curvature?"

Top 10 Reasons Hockey Is the Best Pastime

10. Hockey is the last remnant of the Roman Coliseum rulebook without actually having to sit through pro wrestling.

9. Baseball. Get serious.

8. Real men don't wear figure skates.

7. Golf. Hmm... This one's a toss up. Both sports involve knocking a hard rubber object into a target with a carbon-graphite stick while wearing hideous clothing.

6. Cinemas, while somehow just as cold as hockey arenas, just don't command the same enthusiasm. (And there's no funky chicken in a cinema!)

5. Better sound effects than even the coolest video game.

4. Boxing is arguably the same sport, but those wimps do it *without* skates.

3. Just not enough violence in football.

2. Stamp-collecting is for referees.

1. When's the last time you went to the ballet and had a really good fight break out?

Top 25 Reasons Hockey Is Better than Sex

25. It's okay to bleed during play.

24. If it's a bad game, you can call a time out.

23. Every player usually has two or three sticks to choose from.

22. There is a limit to the size of all equipment.

21. You can still play when you get married.

20. You can change on the fly.

19. Anytime you see an open net, you can go for it.

18. If you can't get it up, who cares?

17. You can score on all the teams in the league, over and over.

16. You can pull the goalie without getting yelled at!

15. It is broadcast live on TV.

14. Everyone can shoot at the same goal.

13. You can shoot into the goal, and it's a good thing!

12. Because of the face mask, nothing can get in your eyes!

11. You always know how big the stick is.

10. It's legal to play hockey professionally.

9. The puck is always hard.

8. Protective equipment is reusable, and you don't even have to wash it.

7. It lasts a full hour.

6. You know you're finished when the buzzer sounds.

5. Your parents cheer when you score.

4. When you're tired, you're supposed to get off and let a buddy take your place.

3. You can count on it at least twice a week.

2. You can tell your friends about it afterwards.

And, the number one reason hockey is better than sex…

1. A two-on-one or three-on-one is not uncommon.

Top 10 Ways the Pittsburgh Penguins Spent Their Time Off After Winning the Stanley Cup

10. Joyriding on the Zamboni.

9. Skeet shooting on the White House lawn.

8. Watching *Oprah*.

7. You know that adorable skating bunny in the Ice Capades? That was me!

6. Watched tape of 2009 playoffs 7000 times.

5. Crank calling Alexander Ovechkin.

4. Playing golf with the Toronto Maple Leafs.

3. Eating!

2. Keeping my stick waxed, if you know what I mean.

1. Doing Stanley Cup-sized Jello shots.

Top 10 Gifts to Give a Goaltender

10. "I got you a Halloween costume, but I see you already have one."

9. Hugs are always welcome.

8. Clothes that bring out the colour of his bruises.

7. Patrick Roy's newest book: *How to Alienate an Entire City in One Easy Step.*

6. Dominik Hasek's goaltending guide: *Ugly Goaltending Made Easy.*

5. Bigger defenseman.

4. Ice packs, ice packs, ice packs!

3. Chia Pet.

2. SPF 50 sunscreen, for that red-light burn on the back of his neck.

1. Free sessions with a psychiatrist.

Three Things Canadians Can't Live Without

1. Hockey

2. Rush

3. Maple syrup

Leafs Acronym

Losers...**E**ven...**A**fter...**F**orty...**S**easons (will still work when they haven't won a Cup after 50 years).

Real-life Hockey Language Dictionary

Blue line: mark on ribcage from leaning over bar, replaying game

Check: piece of paper with about 20 zeroes, delivered weekly to Mats Sundin

Chopper: favoured stick manoeuvre of Chris Pronger and Scott Neidermeyer

Conference: what on-ice officials need to have before they can make any important decision

Crease: prominent piece of Pat Quinn's anatomy

Division: mathematical concept beyond grasp of most Canadian fans

Europeans: skilled players who refuse to watch "Coach's Corner"

Hard worker: player who lacks in the talent department

Hockey Night in Canada **(a.k.a. Hockey Night in Toronto [COTU]):** The Canadian equivalent of what in other countries is known as "Saturday evening." Every *Hockey Night* from October until April, Canadians sit glued to their television sets watching the comedy team known as Don Cherry and straight man Ron MacLean, interspersed with 20-minute intermissions known as ice hockey. *Hockey Night* slows down to every second evening in the spring during the Stanley Cup playoffs. Translation to American: Monday Night Football.

Hooking: what the gal in the thigh-length boots up in Section 14 does for a living

Instant replay: new electronic method for proving on-ice officials' incompetence

One-timer: number of occasions on which Brian Burke has admitted he was wrong

Penalty box: good place for TV close-ups of players mouthing the "F" word at each other

PIMs: rating system for unskilled players

Scoreboard: place for annoying company signs and logos

Shoot: what religious players say after missing wide-open net

Slapshot: movie poking fun at Canada's national pastime

Stanley Cup: trophy awarded to championship team just prior to opening of training camp

Referee: guy in striped shirt who's awfully glad he's not a linesman

Rink: weekend hangout for parents

Roll of tape: what the Canadiens got in the Roy trade

Wraparound: visors worn by Europeans, which piss off Don Cherry

Zamboni: machine used to fill arena with noxious, poisonous fumes

Hockey Player Double Entendre

When the Brunette grabbed his Peca, she just couldn't stop Tugnutt. Excitedly, she screamed, "Holik cow, your Wiemer is Luongo and Fata. Bonk me now and make it Messier!"

You Know You Watch Too Much Hockey When...

❏ You think about what every sport would be like with a hockey stick.

❏ You can impersonate every player.

❏ You can name the top 100 players but can't remember your kids' names.

❏ You keep track of every statistic of every player along with their ranking and ranking points but can't ace statistics in school.

❏ You name your kids after pros.

❏ You are taking an exam, and you are drawing out the line-ups for the next game.

You Know You Play Too Much Hockey When...

❏ You know you play too much hockey when you body check your kid brother.

❏ You call the referee whenever there is an argument.

❏ Instead of fighting the guy who stole your girl-friend, you challenge him to a game of floor hockey.

❏ You are sitting in the arena right now reading this.

The Hockey Fan Checklist

❏ You find stitches and broken noses attractive.

❏ You speak fluent Canadian, even though you've never been within 1000 miles of the border.

❏ You only watch the hockey parts of *Happy Gilmore*.

❏ You hear "Welcome to the Jungle" every time a song comes on, no matter what it is.

❏ You think there are three periods in a basketball game.

❏ You show up at games three hours early.

❏ You cried when Wayne Gretzky retired.

❏ You buy season tickets when you can't afford them.

❏ You refer to every player on the roster by his nickname and know every pre-game ritual.

❏ You use a hockey puck as a paperweight.

❏ You consider taking your vacation time to attend every All-Star Weekend within reach.

❏ You consider body checking obnoxious customers at work when they ask stupid questions.

❏ You aren't ashamed to admit that you've seen all the *Mighty Ducks* movies and can recite key parts ("Goalie's bored, Fulton scored...").

❏ You know which referees are biased against your team.

❏ You are planning road trips for away games, and the schedule isn't out yet.

Descriptions of Team Positions

TEAM COACH
Leaps tall buildings in a single bound
Is more powerful than a locomotive
Is faster than a speeding bullet
Walks on water
Gives policy to God

TEAM CAPTAIN
Leaps short buildings with single bound
Is more powerful than a switch engine
Is just as fast as a speeding bullet
Walks on water if the sea is calm
Talks with God

ASSISTANT CAPTAIN
Leaps short buildings with a running start and
favourable winds
Is almost as powerful as a switch engine
Is faster than a speeding BB
Walks on water in an indoor swimming pool
Talks with God if special request is granted

DEFENCEMAN
Barely clears a Quonset hut
Loses tug-of-war with a switch engine
Can fire a speeding bullet
Swims well
Is occasionally addressed by God

FORWARD
Makes high marks on the wall when trying to leap buildings
Is run over by a locomotive
Can sometimes handle a gun without inflicting self-injury
Dog paddles
Talks to animals

ROOKIE
Runs into buildings
Recognizes locomotive two out of three times
Is not issued ammunition
Can't stay afloat with a life preserver
Talks to walls

REFEREE
Falls over doorsteps when trying to enter buildings
Says "Look at the choo-choo!"
Wets himself with a water pistol
Plays in mud puddles
Mumbles to himself

GOALIE
Lifts buildings and walks under them
Kicks locomotives off the tracks
Catches speeding bullets with his teeth and eats them
Freezes water with a single glance (who needs a Zamboni?)
He IS God

Top Five Things in Hockey that Sound Dirty

5. Slap it!

4. Your jock is bigger than mine.

3. I scored three times.

2. Always wear your protection.

1. PUCK!

Top 10 Uses For a Zamboni

10. Tie rookies up and drag them around the rink.

9. Chasing squirrels around the arena parking lot after practice.

8. Get a couple of them and DRAG!

7. Doin' donuts at the face-off circles.

6. "Just wait until the next time Coach makes me mad!"

5. "Aw, Coach, I was just doing my Jeff Gordon impression.'

4. Scaring the heck out of ice-level broadcasters and analysts.

3. "I just need it to smooth off my lake at home."

2. Provides a moving target for slap-shot practice.

1. CAN YOU SAY "ZAMBONI GIRL"?!

You might be a Puckbunny If...

❏ You arrange your hockey card collection in order of cuteness.

- ❑ Your team is eliminated from the playoffs, so you root for Vancouver "because Mats Sundin is a stud!"
- ❑ You sometimes wonder why they don't make hockey versions of *Bop* and *Tiger Beat*.
- ❑ You think NHL stands for "National Hottie League."
- ❑ You wonder why Jeremy Stevenson and Mike LeClerc don't get called up more often.
- ❑ You have a lot of respect for Sergei Fedorov.
- ❑ You consider Josee Theodore to be one of the greats.
- ❑ You "hate that guy from *Billy Madison*, but the guy in *Happy Gilmore*? Now there's a stud!"
- ❑ You think that Rocket Richard is Buzz Lightyear's cousin from *Toy Story*.
- ❑ You pick Paul Kariya over Georges Laraque in a fight to the death.
- ❑ You can't understand why so many people booed Matt Barnaby and Darius Kasparaitis.
- ❑ You wonder what all the fuss about this "Sidney Crosby" guy is.
- ❑ Your pre-game ritual includes Wash 'N Curl.
- ❑ You wish they'd quit wasting valuable hottie-watching time letting "those slow-moving, ice cream trucks drive around the ice during half-time. I mean nobody ever buys anything!"
- ❑ You list "hockey players" as a hobby.
- ❑ You've used the words "Mark Messier" and "huggable" in the same sentence.
- ❑ You don't find a single thing on this list funny!

Decoder

At last, hockey's secret code has been cracked.
Everyone knows hockey coaches speak in code.
After years of exhaustive study, that code has been
broken. Usually, the coach speaks in code when he's
trying to sugar-coat his assessment of a player or his
team. We now know the difference between what a
coach says and what a coach really means. Here's a
list of the most common code phrases used by
coaches:

Code: He's a role player.
Translation: We think he can play a role; we just
haven't figure out what that role is yet.

Code: He's a "character" guy.
Translation: He makes us laugh, tells jokes and does
impressions.

Code: He's good in the room.
Translation: We should leave him in the room
because he's useless on the ice.

Code: He brings intangibles.
Translation: We're not sure what he brings to the
team.

Code: He's a competitor.
Translation: He competes every night; he just
doesn't win very often.

Code: He's gritty.
Translation: He needs a bath.

Code: He's hard-nosed.
Translation: He's dumb enough to lead with his
face.

Code: He's good in the corners.
Translation: He belongs in the corner—with a dunce
cap on.

Code: He gives us physical presence.
Translation: He takes up space.

Code: He's a technically sound goalie.
Translation: His reflexes are lousy.

Code: He's a reflex goalie.
Translation: He hasn't got a clue how to play the
angles.

Code: He's a power-play specialist.
Translation: I like having an extra man out there to
cover for his screw-ups.

Code: He's a stay-at-home defenseman.
Translation: He can't skate and carry the puck at the
same time.

Code: He's an offensive defenseman.
Translation: He can't play defence.

Code: He adds toughness.
Translation: He's here for two shifts a night and starts fights on both of them.

Code: He's an all-round player.
Translation: He doesn't do anything particularly well.

Code: He's feisty.
Translation: He chirps at the opposition and takes dumb penalties at crucial times.

Code: He's got experience.
Translation: He's lost with better teams.

Code: He has tremendous upside.
Translation: He can't get any worse.

Code: He's a "project."
Translation: This guy was abandoned in the jungle as a small boy and taught to play hockey by the family of gorillas that adopted him. And I'm supposed to coach this?

Code: He's a grinder.
Translation: It's 50-50 he'll miss an empty net from three feet.

Code: He's got good work ethic.
Translation: He works hard but accomplishes little.

Code: He's a playmaker.
Translation: He had better pass, because he shoots like my grandmother.

Code: We've got good chemistry.
Translation: We may be lousy, but we all get along.

Code: We're rebuilding.
Translation: We stink this year and probably will the year after that, too.

Code: We're shaking up the lines to add offense.
Translation: I'm pulling names out of a hat and hoping it works.

Code: We're letting him see the game from above so he can learn.
Translation: He pissed me off so much the last game that I want him as far away from me as possible

Code: We only had a few bright spots tonight.
Translation: I watched my career as a coach go down the crapper.

Code: Things are turning around for us, now.
Translation: We don't suck as much as before, and I can keep my dinner down watching these losers.

Code: He's our star.
Translation: He can actually play hockey.

Code: We don't want to rush him.
Translation: He sucks.

Code: We played undisciplined hockey.
Translation: The ref sucked.

Code: We were not as good as we should be.
Translation: How can these high school dropouts get paid millions for that crap they spewed on the ice tonight?

Code: We need to work harder.
Translation: No more all-night benders the night before a game.

Code: I am in the best shape of my career.
Translation: I have a no-trade clause in my contract.

Carnac the Magnificent

What nobody knows is that, a few years ago, I was able to spend some time with Carnac the Magnificent. He taught me the secrets of psychic prediction, but I was only ever able to master the art so long as it involved images that came in threes. Here, now, are some of my hockey-related psychic readings. Each list of three items is followed by the thing that my amazing abilities have revealed ties them together.

1. Britney Spears and her children
2. Dennis Kucinich and the White House
3. A Kings fan and the Stanley Cup

☞ **Three people dreaming about something they can't have!**

1. Raw Steak
2. Fireworks
3. Gary Bettman

☞ **Three things that should be fired!**

1. Mike Ricci with severe acne
2. Mike Ricci with a broken nose
3. Anze Kopitar

☞ **Three things uglier than Mike Ricci!**

1. A snowman
2. Outdoor ice rinks
3. The San Jose Sharks

☞ **Three things that don't do well after April!**

1. A vermin-infested landfill
2. The nasty inside of a septic tank
3. The uninhabitable toxic surface of Venus

☞ **Three nicer places to live than Edmonton!**

1. Hellen Keller
2. Stevie Wonder
3. Louis Braille

☛ **Three people who could officiate a hockey game better than Mick McGeough!**

1. Napoleon into Russia in winter
2. The Titanic into an iceberg
3. The Winnipeg Jets to Phoenix

☛ **Three of the worst moves of all time!**

1. Benedict Arnold
2. Julius and Ethel Rosenberg
3. Paul Kariya

☛ **I think I'll let you figure this one out!**

1. A small child and a handgun
2. A diabetic and a chocolate cake
3. A Canucks fan and an Internet connection

☛ **Three people who have something they shouldn't!**

1. Being devoured by a pack of wolves
2. Suffering from multiple stab wounds to the eyes
3. Rolling around in a pile of salt after being set on fire

☛ **Three things less painful than a George Parros uppercut!**

1. *Die Hard*
2. *Die Harder*
3. *Die Hard With a Vengeance*
☛ The last three Senators playoff runs!

1. A terrible movie theatre
2. Upper deck seats at Honda Centre
3. The 2006–2007 Buffalo Sabres
☛ Three things that should have Cup holders but don't!

1. Paint drying
2. Grass growing
3. Water boiling
☛ Three things more exciting to watch than the New Jersey Devils!

1. Helping an elderly person cross the street
2. Holding the door open for an attractive person
3. How referees officiate Red Wing games
☛ Three examples of "Special Consideration"!

1. A pile of garbage
2. A corpse
3. The Toronto Maple Leafs
☛ Three things that don't stink any less after 40 years!

1. The death of Elvis
2. George W. Bush is inaugurated as President of the U.S.
3. The Florida Panthers reaching the 1996 Stanley Cup Final

☛ **Three things people still can't believe actually happened!**

1. A large crocodile
2. A river in Egypt
3. Daniel Alfredsson saying he didn't shoot the puck at Neidermayer in Game Four of the Stanley Cup Final

☛ **Three examples of denial!**

1. A circumcision
2. Dan Cloutier's goaltending
3. Don Cherry's wardrobe

☛ **Three things that are painful to look at!**

1. Brad Pitt's atrocious gas
2. Colin Farrell's horrible foot odour
3. Ryan Getzlaf's bald spot

☛ **Three things that still fail to keep the ladies away!**

1. A necktie made of barbed wire
2. A bucket full of meat in a lion's den
3. A 50-pound backpack while hiking uphill
☞ **Three things that I'd rather wear than the new Stars' jerseys!**

1. Cabernet Sauvignon
2. Pinot Grigio
3. Sidney Crosby
☞ **Three types of "whine"!**

1. A telemarketer
2. A convicted felon
3. A high school dropout
☞ **Three things you would rather have your child become than an Avalanche fan!**

1. Leonardo of the TMNT
2. Bowser Koopa of Super Mario Brothers
3. Sean Avery of the New York Rangers
☞ **Three famous turtles!**

The NHL might be creating a new contest to energize its fans. How does it work? The first fan to actually locate a channel airing an NHL playoff game wins.

You Might be Addicted to Hockey If...

❏ You deck the guy who says, "Check, please."

❏ You think your city's red-light district is around the opposing goal.

❏ You own a Zamboni.

❏ You keep your Zamboni in the garage and your main car in the driveway.

❏ Your calendar only runs from October to June.

❏ You wonder how you will get through July, August and September.

❏ The Hanson Brothers are your favourite actors.

❏ You wonder when the Hanson Brothers started a singing career.

❏ You punish your kids with "minors," "majors" and "misconducts."

❏ You name your first son "Sidney."

❏ When someone says "two minutes," you respond, "What for?!"

❏ When you hear a siren in traffic, you wonder who scored and who got the assist.

❏ You get bored at an ice-skating show because there are no fights.

More You Know You're a Hockey Fan When...

❏ Your idea of serving breakfast is giving each of your kids a fork and dropping an egg in the middle of the table.

❏ When you come to a traffic signal and the light turns green, you stop.

❏ When you come to a traffic signal and the light turns red, you get really excited and start cheering.

❏ You consider the Forum in Montréal a place of worship.

❏ You keep a picture of the Stanley Cup in your wallet in front of the picture of your family.

❏ Instead of duct tape, you use hockey tape to fix everything.

❏ You know the difference between "the Garden," "the Gahden" and "the Gardens."

❏ You call a trip to the Hockey Hall of Fame a "pilgrimage."

❏ You think the Canadian National Anthem is the theme from *Hockey Night in Canada*.

❏ You send Gordie Howe a birthday card yet can't remember your own family members' birthdays.

❏ All your kids are either named Gordie, Bobby or Sidney.

❏ You went to see *West Side Story* because you thought it was about a game between Vancouver and San Jose.

❏ You went into a bank that advertised "Free Checking" and walked out disappointed.

❏ When someone refers to "the Classics," you think they're talking about the "Original Six."

❑ Your cure for everything is a couple of extra-strength aspirin and a shot of novocaine.

❑ You can pronounce anything in French, yet you have no idea what it means.

❑ You can say "Khabibulin," "Tkachuk," "Jagr," "Leschyshyn" and "Tverdovsky" without getting tongue-tied.

❑ Every time you see the name Roy, you automatically pronounce it "Wah."

❑ You're no longer allowed to play chess because you misunderstand the meaning of the word "check."

❑ You think the four food groups are nachos, beer, pretzels and rubber.

❑ Everything in your wardrobe is in your team's colours.

❑ You still remember which teams were in the Patrick, Smythe, Norris and Adams divisions and which divisions were in the Campbell and Prince of Wales conferences.

❑ You know the difference between "The Edmonton Express" and "The Human Express."

❑ You refer to your team's enforcers as "chippy players," and you refer to other teams' enforcers as "freaking little pieces of monkey &*%$£"#@."

❑ When you're at a game, you're not bothered when your kid cusses, but when he says "shutout" before the game is over, you threaten to wash his mouth out with soap.

❑ You wonder what Miroslav Satan did to become the Prince of Darkness and Ruler of Hell.

❑ You think the proper way to spell the plural of "leaf" is "leafs."

❑ You can name all the Sutter brothers in order.

❑ Your closet is divided into two sections: HOME and AWAY.

How to Have Fun as a Ref

When you're a ref, you have to face the fact that everyone hates you. The fans hate you, the players hate you and the owners hate you. If you're a referee, you're about as popular as a rattlesnake in a lucky dip. There is only one way to stay sane and happy as a referee. It's not about love of the sport, and it's not about impartiality. It's all about knowing how much you're hated and getting revenge. The best way to do this is to get your retaliation first. Here are my rules for having a fun, relaxing and, above all, vengeful time as a referee:

1) Never read any interviews with players. They tend to criticize the standard of refereeing in this country, and you really don't need to see that kind of thing.

2) Decide on your penalty ratio. This is the ratio of penalties during the game compared to the number of times you actually blow your whistle. Most NHL referees think a penalty ratio of 3:1 keeps the game flowing and saves them having to work too hard.

3) Change your first name to "Ohgodits," then when you skate onto the ice at the beginning of a match and half the crowd says "Oh god, it's Smith" (assuming your name is Smith), it'll just sound like they're shouting your name.

4) In the referee's dressing room before the game, toss a coin and decide which side you're going to show bias toward. It really winds the fans up. Note: you may want to simply choose the away side, so that all the home fans will get wound up at you. They are a much larger—and therefore more satisfying—group to anger.

5) Never wave at the fans when you skate out before the match. It only upsets them.

6) Practice ignoring people. The fans will shout at you, and the players will shout at you, and it's best if you can ignore all of them. (Referees still living at home with their mothers feel that this is a very valuable skill and have plenty of chance to practice it.)

7) Read the rules, but don't bother too much about learning them fully or strictly enforcing them. Applying them randomly (such as penalizing people for being offside when they aren't) is much more fun and another good wind-up for fans and players alike.

8) Learn to skate with your eyes shut. This will allow you to miss penalties and help to keep up that penalty ratio. If this is too hard, just keep your eyes on the attractive young ladies in the

front rows of the crowd. (It might be the closest you'll ever get to an attractive woman.)

9) If you do have to penalize someone, make the penalties as irrational and arbitrary as you like. Five-plus games for a minor unsportsmanlike is a wonderful wind-up. Two minutes for a savage boarding that leaves a player concussed is also very satisfying.

10) If one player fouls another, and the fouled player retaliates, penalize him harder than the player committing the foul. If you really want to wind people up, don't penalize that player at all, just the victim.

11) Try to get in the way when a player hits the puck along the boards. It can introduce a wonderful random element to the game and wind people up again.

12) Park your car where you can make a quick get-away from the arena after the match. If the fans start recognizing it, hire one for match nights.

Twenty Fun Things to Do If You're a Goalie

1. One word: salt.

2. Before the game, secretly switch the green and red light bulbs around.

3. Slash, hook and spear every opposing player who comes within three feet of your crease, then point and laugh at your teammates when they have to go to the box for you.

4. After you cover the puck and the ref blows the whistle, quickly put the puck in your shorts before the ref can pick it up. Tell him to "comegetit."

5. Moon the goal cam.

6. Get into a shouting match with your stick. Then tell the ref you refuse to play until the stick apologizes.

7. If you're on the bench, start giving away all the sticks on the rack to the fans sitting behind you.

8. Every time an announcement is made over the PA system, drop to your knees and start scream-ing, "Not the voices again!"

9. Every time the opposing team scores, remove one piece of your equipment.

10. Fill your teammates' water bottles with vodka and watch the fun.

11. As soon as the trainers finish putting your equipment on you, say out loud, "Hey, you know what astronauts can do right in their suits?" Then watch the fun as they scramble to pull the equipment off again.

12. During a faceoff, stand next to your defensemen, as if you're a skater, too.

13. When someone scores a hat trick, grab as many hats off the ice as you can and stuff them in your jersey.

14. Using hockey tape, put a large bull's eye in the middle of your chest.

15. Using hockey tape, put "(insert name of opponent's enforcer here) Sucks" on the back of your teammates' jerseys.

16. Rub Ben Gay on the inside of your teammates' cups.

17. Pour Krazy Glue inside your teammates' cups.

18. When the trainer isn't looking, throw a red sock in the washer with the white home jerseys. (But make sure you take yours out!)

19. Before the game starts, go up to the opposing team, start crying and say, "Please don't score on me! My coach beats me if I let a puck in!" Then, when the ref comes to take you back to your crease, start screaming, "No! I don't wanna go! I don't wanna go!"

20. Position yourself in front of the goal cam and proceed to scratch your rear end.

2009–2012 Expansion: HOLD IT

Despite all of the failed expansion teams, the NHL is considering adding 10 more hockey teams. So, would you like to own a National Hockey League team?

All you need is $2 billion dollars and a wife, whom everyone is allowed to play with!

You must choose a colour that the rest of the league will hate (not including the mandatory pink!), and you must choose a team name that is offensive to all religious groups.

City size does not matter, as long as you can afford the bill! *Good luck!*

However, the city must be located in a region that does not receive any ice or snow. Otherwise, the team will be fined $100 million for every inch of snow that falls.

Even attempting to place a team in Canada will make Gary Bettman cry. He will sue you for enough money to create another team in a warm-climate city, where nobody has ever heard of hockey.

It's worth choosing a logo that people can make fun of, because you can have fun screwing a poor bastard out of as much money as possible to wear the ugly thing.

In Case of Another Strike

THE NHL PLAYER-ADOPTION PROGRAM NEEDS YOU!

With an NHL players' strike against the team owners looming, now is the time for us to show the world just how much we care. It's just not right. Hundreds of hockey players in our very own country are living at or just below the seven-figure salary level! Atrocious! And, as if that weren't bad enough, they will be deprived of pay for several weeks—possibly a whole year—as a result of the strike. But now you can help! For about $2000 a day—that's less than the cost of a large-screen projection TV—you can help a hockey player remain economically viable during his time of need.

Two thousand dollars a day may not seem like a lot of money to you, but to a hockey player, it could mean the difference between a vacation spent golfing in Florida or a Mediterranean cruise. For you, $2000 is nothing more than three months' rent or mortgage payments. But to a hockey player, $2000 a day will only just replace his salary.

Your commitment of $2000 a day will enable a player to buy that home entertainment centre, trade in the year-old Lexus for a new Ferrari or enjoy a weekend in Rio.

"HOW WILL I KNOW I'M HELPING?"

Each month, you will receive a complete financial report on the player you sponsor. Detailed information about his stocks, bonds, real estate and other investment holdings will be mailed to your home. You'll also get information on how he plans to invest the $5-million lump sum he will receive upon retirement. Plus, upon signing up for this program, you will receive a photo of the player (unsigned). Put the photo on your refrigerator to remind you of other people's suffering.

"HOW WILL HE KNOW I'M HELPING?"

Your hockey player will be told that he has a SPECIAL FRIEND who wants to help in his time of need. Although the player won't know your name, he will be able to make collect calls to your home via a special operator, just in case additional funds are needed for unexpected expenses.

Simply fill out the form below.

———— YES, I want to help!

I would like to sponsor a striking NHL player.
My preference is checked below:

☐ Starter   ☐ Reserve   ☐ Star*

☐ Superstar**   ☐ Entire team***

☐ I'll sponsor a player most in need. Please select
one for me.

* Higher cost
** Much higher cost
***Please call our 1-900 number to ask for the cost of a specific team
(Sorry, does not include cheerleaders)

Please charge the account listed below $2054.79 per day
for a reserve player or starter for the duration of the
strike. Please send me a picture of the player I have sponsored, along with a team logo and my very own NHL
Players Association badge to wear proudly on my lapel.

☐ Master Card   ☐ Visa

☐ American Express   ☐ Discover Card

☐ Diner's Club

Your Name: _____

Telephone Number: _____

Account Number:_____

Exp. Date: _____

Signature: _____

Mail completed form to NHL Players Association or call 1-888-TOO-MUCH
now to enrol by phone. (Children under 18 must have parental approval.)

Note: Sponsors are not permitted to contact the player they have sponsored, either in person or by other means including, but not limited to,
telephone calls, letters, e-mail or third parties. Keep in mind that the
hockey player you have sponsored will be much too busy enjoying his free
time, thanks to your generous donations. Oh yes, contributions are not tax-
deductible.

Puns and Limericks

The ref keeps shafting us the offsides; I think he's *blue lyin'*.

In later years was the Great One in decline? Yes he was on the *Wayne*.

In Québec, they used to practice throwing the puck in the zone and then sitting back to wait for a turnover. But eventually the players were criticized for this *dump-and-chaise* tactic.

Can linesmen enter the Hall of Fame? Yes, because they decide who's *HOFside*.

Where did the Flopper work in the offseason? At *Dominik's Hat Check*.

Which local sportswriters are most effusive? Those who work in the *praise box*!

After the Moroccan scored a hat trick, the players gathered for the *fez-off*.

The coddled superstar sat in the seats with the fans instead of on the bench with the team; for this, ironically enough, he was accused of *grandstanding*!

What type of films should players watch to improve their shot? *Slap stick*.

Where's the weak spot on a Scottish goalie? The *fief hole*.

Which Oiler great had a soft spot for Indian food? *Jari Curry*.

If Messier retires he's sure to be *moosed*.

There once was a sport on the ice
Where Canadians and Yankees played nice
But I think it's extinct
Though the Rangers still stink
Cause the owners couldn't get a fair price.

The Habs were having a fight
The game was incredibly tight
The fans stood and roared
When they evened the score
Now one more and we'll say *au revoir*.

The Red Wings this year have been cracking
And certainly haven't been slacking
So let's make some noise

For Tim and the boys
And send them Canadien Habs packing.

You may think that I'm an old crony
But I'd love to drive a Zamboni.
To glide 'cross the ice
Would be really nice
Eating pizza with hot pepperoni.

So when planning a night out, just think,
"Where's the action, the buzz and a drink?"
And whether young or old,
Come in from the cold
For a warm welcome at your local rink.

List of Hockey Movies
King of Hockey **(1936)**

Dick Purcell, Anne Nagel, Wayne Morris, George E. Stone, Joseph Crehan, Ann Gillis, Gordon Hart, Dora Clement, Guy Usher, Garry Owen, Max Hoffman Jr., George Beranger, Frank Faylen, Frank Bruno, Harry Davenport.

Gamblers try to get star hockey player Gabby Dugan to throw games. Purcell was on the Fordham University hockey team. Other players are from the University of Southern California and Loyola University hockey teams.

Idol of the Crowds (1937)
John Wayne, Sheila Bromley, George Lloyd.

A retired hockey player makes a comeback to earn money to improve his chicken farm. Just before the championship series, he is offered a bribe to throw the games. Some wooden dialogue, but it's John Wayne!

The Game That Kills (1937)
Charles Quigley, Rita Hayworth, J. Farrell Mac-Donald, Arthur Loft, John Gallaudet, Clyde Dilson.

The star left wing of the Indians hockey team is killed during a game with two of his own team-mates under mysterious circumstances. His brother tries to bring his killers to justice.

It's A Pleasure! (1945)
Sonja Henie, Michael O'Shea, Marie McDonald, Bill Johnson, Gus Schilling, Iris Adrian, Arthur Loft.

Don Martin is a star Wildcats hockey player who is thrown out of the league for hitting a referee. He subsequently gets a job with Buzz Fletcher's ice show, marries the star but then loses her. Henie's precision skating is the highlight of the film, of course. Henie won three Olympic gold medals in figure skating between 1928 and 1936.

White Lightning (1953)
Stanley Clements, Barbara Bestar, Steve Brodie, Gloria Blondell, Lyle Talbot, Lee Van Cleef.

The Red Devils hockey team is losing because gamblers are paying off the star player. But a boyhood friend joins the team and sets him straight. Along the way, tempers flare over a woman and his arrogant attitude.

Face-Off (1971)

Art Hindle, Trudy Young, Eric Cryderman, John Vernon.

Love story about a Canadian professional hockey player and a folk singer. The story focuses on their attempts to come to terms with career and lifestyle differences. Shot in and around Toronto, the film includes vintage NHL footage. Former pros George Armstrong and Derek Sanderson appear as themselves.

Paperback Hero (1973)

Keir Dullea, Elizabeth Ashley, John Beck, Dayle Haddon.

Saskatchewan hockey star is popular with the ladies but fantasizes he's a western gunslinger. Better than it sounds.

Slap Shot (1977)

Paul Newman, Strother Martin, Michael Ontkean, Jennifer Warren, Lindsay Crouse, Jerry Houser.

Newman is the player-coach of the Federal League Charlestown Chiefs, a minor league team going nowhere. Average script picks up with the arrival of the bespectacled Hanson brothers who inspire the team to play dirty to win. Still the best hockey movie ever made, but it has way too much profanity for the kids. The Hanson Brothers went on to play minor league hockey and in the NHL. The filming was scheduled to take place in the off-season, but brother Jack got called up because Edmonton made the playoffs. Dave Hanson took Jack's place, and Jerry Houser was cast to play Dave's original role, "Dave 'Killer' Carlson." (*The Official Home of the Hanson Brothers*, Steve Carlson, Jeff Carlson, Dave Hanson.)

The Deadliest Season (1977)
  Michael Moriarty, Kevin Conway, Meryl Streep, Paul D'Amato, Sully Boyar, Jill Eikenberry, Andrew Duggan.

  TV movie exposes greedy promoters as the profiteers of violence they really are. This is *Slap Shot* played straight, as an aggressive player is brought up on charges of manslaughter after critically injuring a rival player (his best friend). Excellent hard-hitting script is well acted, but unfortunately, Moriarty is miscast in the lead. Also notable for Streep's film debut.

The Boy Who Drank Too Much (1980)
  Scott Baio, Lance Kerwin, Ed Lauter, Don Murray, Ron Max.

  Buff Saunders is a high school hockey player fighting a drinking problem.

Miracle on Ice (1981)

Karl Malden, Andrew Stevens, Steve Guttenberg, Jerry Houser, Jessica Walter.

TV movie about the U.S. hockey team's gold medal victory at the 1980 Lake Placid Olympics. Average story but enjoyable hockey scenes. Malden plays Coach Herb Brooks convincingly.

Hockeyfeber (1983)

A Norwegian hockey team, loaded with conflicts on and off the ice, hires the Finnish coach to whip them into shape. The team in the movie, Manglerud Star, is an actual Norwegian hockey team. Translated, the title means *Hockey Fever*.

Hockey Night (1984)

Megan Follows, Rick Moranis, Gail Youngs.

A female goalie makes the boys' Canadian hockey team. A nice little film suitable for the whole family to watch. Moranis also stars in football's *Little Giants*.

Generation (1985)

Richard Beymer, Hannah Cutrona, Marta DuBois, Drake Hogestyn.

A man invents a new piece of equipment for pro hockey that his brother thinks will cause crippling injuries to the players and destroy the game.

Touch and Go (1986)

Michael Keaton, Maria Conchita Alonoso, Ajay Naidu.

Prima donna hockey star gets mixed up with juvenile delinquent, falls for the boy's mother, and it changes his life. Bland script and typical dialogue hurt entire film, noted only for Keaton's reliable performance.

Youngblood (1986)

Rob Lowe, Cynthia Gibb, Patrick Swayze, Ed Lauter, Jim Youngs, Eric Nesterenko, George Finn, Keanu Reeves.

Passive minor league hockey player Dean Young-blood is forced to deal with a demanding coach and an aggressive rival player. He's also dating the coach's daughter. (She drives the Zamboni, too!) Predictable script, but the hockey sequences aren't bad, with plenty of action between the Hamilton Mustangs and the Thunder Bay Bombers. Reeves, in his acting debut, is the goalie.

The Last Season (1986)

Booth Savage, Deborah Cass.

An ex-NHL player is hired as a coach in Finland.

Brigitte Gall: Joan of Montréal (1990)

Joan runs up against the typical obstacles of trying out as the goalie on a boys' hockey team.

Le Choix (1991)

Patrice Bissonnette, Judith Bérard, Gilbert Sicotte, Marc Messier, Denis Bouchard, Eric Hoziel, Michel Mongeau.

Canadian TV movie.

The Cutting Edge (1992)

D.B. Sweeney, Moira Kelly, Roy Dotrice, Terry O'Quinn.

Injured Olympic hockey star meets Olympic ice skater hopeful and decides to help her win a gold medal in paired figure skating. Unique story idea works, as does the stars' chemistry with each other. Some good skating scenes, too.

The Mighty Ducks (1992)

Emilio Estevez, Lane Smith, Heidi Kling.

Lawyer Gordon Bombay must perform community service by coaching a raw bunch of pee wee hockey players. Disinterested at first, he is motivated by fair play, recruits a couple of new players and turns the team into the Mighty Ducks. As good as *The Bad News Bears* and better than *Little Giants*. Watch this with the kids. Cameos by Dallas Stars Basil McRae and Mike Modano.

Gross Misconduct (1993)

Daniel Kash, Peter MacNeill, Linda Goranson, Dough Hughes, Lenore Zann.

The story of former NHL left-winger Brian "Spinner" Spencer. Spencer's saga is one of a life of violence. (He was shot to death at age 39.) Spencer is shown in archival footage. Based on the book of the same title by Martin O'Malley.

Airborne (1993)

Shane McDermott, Seth Green, Brittney Powell, Edie McClurg, Patrick O'Brien, Chris Conrad.

A teenage surfer from California has to stay with his aunt, uncle and cousin in Cincinnati. He immediately gets on the bad side of the high school hockey players until they learn he is a very good inline rollerblader. Pass.

D2: The Mighty Ducks (1994)

Emilio Estevez, Kathryn Erbe, Michael Tucker.

The Ducks get a chance to play in the Junior Goodwill games representing their country as Team U.S.A. Not as good as the original, but the kids will still like it. Several cameos, including Wayne Gretzky and Karim Abdul-Jabbar. Ducks fly together.

Net Worth (1995)

Aidan Devine, Kevin John Conway, Robin Gammell, Carl Marotte, Richard Donat, Dan Lett, Michael J. Reynolds.

Canadian TV movie based on the true story of Detroit Red Wings player Ted Lindsay attempt to organize the first players' union in 1955. Other principals in the story include Gordie Howe, owners Conn Smythe, Jimmy Norris and Bruce Norris, coach Jack Adams, and NHL commissioner Clarence

Campbell. Most of the story is off the ice, but the recreated hockey scenes are realistic. From the book by David Cruise and Alison Griffiths.

Sudden Death **(1995)**
Jean-Claude Van Damme, Powers Boothe, Raymond J. Barry.

Below-average story of the vice-president being held hostage during the Stanley Cup Finals in Pittsburgh. Lots of action and special effects, though.

D3: The Mighty Ducks **(1996)**
Emilio Estevez, Jeffrey Nordling, Joshua Jackson.

The Ducks win a scholarship with a chance to play hockey at an elite private school for a new coach. Strictly for the kids.

Les Boys **(1997)**
Marc Messier, Remy Girard, Patrick Huard.

Canadian comedy about an amateur hockey team. Stan, the club owner, owes $50,000 to Méo, so his team helps him out. Followed by three sequels.

The Sheldon Kennedy Story **(1999)**
Jonathan Scarfe, Polly Shannon, Robert Wisden.

Kennedy was an NHL player who suffered from sexual abuse as a junior hockey player. He is now a leading advocate against child abuse.

H-E-Double Hockey Sticks! **(1999)**
Will Friedle, Rhea Perlman, Matthew Lawrence.

Disney comedy about an apprentice devil sent by Satan to steal the soul of a young hockey player. Based on the opera *Griffelkin* by Lucas Foss. Strictly for the kids.

Mystery, Alaska (1999)

Russell Crowe, Hank Azaria, Mary McCormack, Burt Reynolds, Colm Meaney, Lolita Davidovich, Maury Chaykin, Ron Eldard, Ryan Northcott.

Comedy about a small town that overreacts when their local hockey team is chosen to play the New York Rangers in a nationally broadcast event. Somewhat entertaining but could've been better. It is too flat and clichéd. Phil Esposito, Barry Melrose, Mike Myers and Little Richard have cameos.

Do You Believe in Miracles? (2001)

Documentary about the U.S. Olympic hockey team's upset victory over the Russians in the 1980 Winter Games. Includes live footage taken at Lake Placid, New York, and interviews with Jim Craig, Mike Eruzione, Jack O'Callahan, coach Herb Brooks, manager Craig Patrick and Russian players Vladislav Tretiak and Boris Mikhailov. There is also commentary by ABC sports broadcasters Al Michaels and Jim Lampley. Four players went on to play in the NHL. Brooks coached four years in the league.

The Rhino Brothers (2001)

Gabrielle Rose, Curtis Bechdholt, Deanna Milligan, William MacDonald.

A story of a Canadian family and one son's journey to play in a professional hockey league. Supported and hindered by his immediate family, he rides an emotional rollercoaster of emotions in the up and down life of a hockey player.

The Demo Crew **(2001)**
John E. Vitali, Susan Blake, Robert Pascucci, Tony Devon, Freddie Ganno.

Anthony Valentine reforms his old gang into a recreational street hockey team. They aren't too enthusiastic, until one of them is killed in a car accident. The players now bond together and become better friends than they've ever been.

Slap Shot 2: Breaking the Ice **(2002)**
Stephen Baldwin, Jessica Steen, Gary Busey, David Hemmings, Hanson Brothers.

A decent sequel, the minor league Chiefs are sold to a new owner with a female coach, placing them in a league in which they regularly lose games to a Globetrotters-like team. Did not receive a theatrical release.

Miracle **(2004)**
Kurt Russell, Eddie Cahill, Michael Mantenuto, Patrick O'Brien Dempsey, Kenneth Mitchell, Nathan West.

The true story of player-turned-coach Herb Brooks (Russell), who led the 1980 U.S. Olympic hockey team in the emotional upset victory over the Russians.

Hockey Mom **(2004)**

Tanya Allen, Colin Campbell, Andrew Chalmers, Jessalyn Gilsig.

Paula Taymore—who once almost made the Olympic team—finds herself drawn into a challenge match against an irritating local men's squad. Fresh from a painful divorce, and doubting herself, Paula must make a winner out of an explosive, irreverent crew of women hockey players who flock to her town, Red Deer Alberta, to assemble the team. AKA "Chicks With Sticks." (From *The Internet Movie Database*)

Maurice Richard **(2005)**

Roy Dupuis.

The story of superstar hockey player Maurice "The Rocket" Richard.

Chapter Nine

Team Humour

"Playing the Leafs is like eating Chinese food. Ten minutes later, you want to play them again."

−Roger Neilson, NHL head coach, on his former team

Mortal Enemies

A Senators fan and a Leafs fan get into a car accident. Both cars are totally demolished, but, amazingly, neither of them are hurt. The Senators fan's car has a Senators sticker clearly visible, and the Leafs fan's car has a Leafs sticker clearly visible.

After they crawl out of their cars, the Leaf fan says, "So, you're a Senators fan. That's interesting. I'm a Leafs fan. Wow! Just look at our cars. There's nothing left, but fortunately, we are unhurt. This must be a sign from God that we should meet and be friends and live together in peace the rest of our days."

The Senators fan replied," I agree with you completely—this must be a sign from God!" The Senators fan continued, "And look at this! Here's another miracle. My car is completely demolished, but this bottle of whisky didn't break. Surely God wants us to drink this and celebrate our good fortune."

Then he hands the bottle to the Leafs fan. The Leafs fan nods his head in agreement, opens the bottle and takes a few big swigs from the bottle, then hands it back to the Senators fan. The Senators fan takes the bottle, puts the cap back on and hands it back to the Leafs fan.

The Leafs fan asks, "Aren't you having any?"

The Senators fan replies, "No. I think I'll just wait for the police."

The Sharks hired Todd McClellan as head coach. They were drawn to him because he was bleeding and looked like an injured seal.

Q: What should the new Montréal Canadiens name be?

A: The Montréal Tampons, because they only last one period and don't have a second string.

Hockey MasterCard commercial:
Bobby Holik: $9M a year

Pavel Bure: $10M a year

Jaromir Jagr: $11M a year

Stanley Cup: PRICELESS

There are some things money can't buy. For everything else, there's the New York Rangers.

Poor Isles

In court the other day was a case regarding the custody of a small child.

The judge asked the boy, "Do you want to live with your mother?"

He replied, "No I don't want to live with her because she beats me!"

The judge then asked, "Do you want to live with your father?"

The boy said, "No he beats me, too."

Finally the judge asked, "Where do you want to live?"

The child responded, "I want to live with the New York Islanders."

The judge asked, "Why do you want to live with the New York Islanders?"

The boy exclaimed, "Because the New York Islanders don't beat anybody."

As part of a promotional gimmick, the Los Angeles Kings decided to have short spelling bee for some first graders at centre ice during an intermission.

The first child was asked to spell "cat."

The child said "C-A-T, cat."

And the Kings fans started yelling, "Aw, come on, give him another chance!"

Toronto Maple Leaf Hunters

A group of players from the Toronto Maple Leafs went on a hunting trip, setting up their camp deep in the woods. As evening came, one of the hunters walked into the camp and, with an uneasy look on his face, asked, "Is everybody here?"

Someone said, "Yes."

Then the exasperated hunter asked, "Nobody's hurt?"

"No."

"Thank god," said the hunter. "That means I shot a deer!"

Hockey Jock Fishing Trip

Two dumb hockey jocks were out fishing in a boat and pulling in fish after fish. They were catching so many fish that their boat quickly filled up, and they had to go back to shore early to unload.

"This is fantastic," said the first man. "We should mark this spot, so we can come here again."

"You're right," said the second man, who then promptly dived over the side and painted a big "X" on the bottom of the boat. Back in the boat, the men confidently headed back to the dock, but, just before they got out of the boat, the second man said, "I just thought of something. What if we don't get the same boat tomorrow?"

Robbery?

Burglars recently broke into the St. Louis Blues' home arena and stole the entire contents of the trophy room. Police are looking for a man carrying a carpet.

Schooled

"He's great on the rink," a sportswriter said of a young Philadelphia Flyers player in a interview with his coach.

"But how's his scholastic work?"

"Why, he makes straight A's," replied the coach.

"Wonderful!" said the sportswriter.

"Yes," agreed the coach, "but his B's are a little crooked."

Did you hear that on the Leafs bus they hooked up a lie detector?

One day, Luke Schenn hooks himself up and says, "I think we have the best defence in the league." Immediately, the detector goes off.

Matt Stajan hooks himself up and says, "I think I'm the best hockey player in the game." Immediately, the lie detector goes off.

Brian Burke steps up and says, "I think," and immediately, the lie detector goes off.

Ticket Incentive

A husband and wife were having dinner at a very fine restaurant, when an absolutely stunning young woman comes over to their table and gives the husband a big open-mouthed kiss and says she'll see him later.

When she walks away, the wife glares at her husband and says, "Who the hell was that?"

"Oh," replies the husband, "she's my mistress."

"That's the last straw," says the wife. "I've had enough. I want a divorce!"

"I can understand that," replies her husband, "but remember, if we get a divorce, it will mean no more shopping trips to Paris, no more wintering in Barbados, no more summers in Tuscany, no more Infiniti or Lexus in the garage.

"I still want a divorce!" says the wife.

"It will also mean there'll be no more Red Wings hockey tickets. Still, the decision is yours," the husband continues.

Just then, a mutual friend enters the restaurant with a gorgeous babe on his arm.

"Who's that woman with Jim?" asks the wife.

"That's his mistress," says her husband.

"Ours is prettier," she replies.

Hotline

The Nashville Predators have apparently set up a call centre for fans who are troubled by their current form. The number is 1-800-10-10-10. Calls charged at peak rate for overseas users. Once again that number is 1-800-won nothing won nothing won nothing.

Good Boy

While attending a Colorado Avalanche game, a guy notices another guy with a dog at his side. To his amazement, when the Avalanche score, the dog does a flip. Again they score, and again the dog does a flip. This goes on three or four times, until the guy finally just can't stand it anymore and has to ask why the dog does a flip every time the team scores.

So, he gets up and goes over to the guy with the dog and says, "Excuse me sir, I have a question about your dog. I noticed that every time the Avalanche score a goal, your dog does a flip. Why?"

The man replies, "I know it's weird, and I have no explanation."

First guy then says, "What does he do when the Avalanche win?"

The guy with the dog replies, "I don't know. I've only had him for 15 years!"

Four prospective owners have applied to buy the Phoenix Coyotes and keep them in Arizona. This is the first time in sports history that a team has more buyers than fans.

Schooled

A first-grade teacher explains to her class that she is a Dallas Stars fan. She asks her students to raise their hands if they are Stars fans, too. All of their hands fly into the air, except for one little girl's.

"Why didn't you raise your hand?" the teacher asks the girl.

"Because I'm not a Stars fan," she replies.

"Then," asks her teacher, "what are you?"

"I'm a proud San Jose Sharks fan," boasts the little girl.

The teacher gets a little red in the face and asks the little girl why she is a Sharks fan.

"Well, my Mom and Dad are Sharks fans, so I'm a Sharks fan, too," she responds.

The teacher is now angry. "That's no reason," she says loudly. "What if your Mom was a meth junkie, and your Dad was inbred. What would you be then?"

The little girl pipes up, "A Dallas Stars fan."

New Names

The Edmonton Oilers have proven that oil and Stanley Cup contenders are both diminishing resources in the Edmonton area. With this theme in mind, I submit the following possible name changes for the Oilers, to better reflect the nature of their play this season.

- ☛ Edmonton Broilers…they're cooked in only 60 minutes.
- ☛ Edmonton Soilers…they stink like a baby's diaper.
- ☛ Edmonton Shorelers…they're all coasters.
- ☛ Edmonton Shoalers…they're buried deep but can be seen briefly at high tide.
- ☛ Edmonton Spoilers…they're past their due date, gone rotten.
- ☛ Edmonton Doily-ers…they play very daintily.
- ☛ Edmonton Doll-ers…you can dress them up like real hockey players, but you know its still pretend.
- ☛ Edmonton Lawyers…their case is pretty weak, and all lawyers suck.
- ☛ Edmonton Voyeur-lers…they like to watch the other teams play for the big one.

☞ Edmonton Coilers…they're just going around in circles.

☞ Edmonton Ships Ahoy-lers…they're on a slow boat to nowhere.

☞ Edmonton Whoa-lers…slowing down.

☞ Edmonton Lowlers…where to find them in the standings.

☞ Edmonton Joy-lers…yeah, maybe when hell freezes over.

Wrong Person

A Flyers fan, a Rangers fan and Pamela Anderson are sitting together in a train travelling to New York City, when the train enters a tunnel and the car goes completely dark. Suddenly, there's a kissing noise and then the sound of a really loud slap.

When the train comes out of the tunnel, Pamela Anderson and the Flyers fan are sitting as if nothing happened. The Rangers fan is holding his slapped face and thinking, "That Flyers fan must have kissed Pamela, and she swung at him and missed, slapping me instead."

Pamela is thinking, "That Rangers fan must have tried to kiss me, accidentally kissed the Flyers fan and got slapped for it."

And the Flyers fan is thinking, "This is great. The next time the train goes through a tunnel, I'll make another kissing noise and slap that stinking Rangers fan again."

Sabres

Two buddies were talking about going to see the Buffalo Sabres on the weekend. One said, "It's pointless even thinking about it. My wife will never let me go."

"It's easy," said his workmate. "All you have to do is pick her up, carry her to the bedroom, fling her on the bed, rip her clothes off, screw her and say, 'I'm going to the game.'"

The two men met up again on the Monday morning. "Did you do what I said?"

"Yeah!" said the other. "A hour before the game, I picked up my wife, carried her to the bedroom and flung her on the bed. Then, as I was pulling off her knickers and unzipping my fly, I thought, "What the hell, the Sabres haven't been playing that well lately."

Leafs Golf Therapy

Out golfing with the Toronto Maple Leafs after another year of missing the playoffs, the team's physical therapist tees off on the golf course. She slices her shot and hits one of the players standing on the adjacent green. The player collapses in agony with his hand pressed firmly between his legs. The physical therapist runs over and says, "Don't worry, I have medical training. I can help reduce the pain."

The player lets her go to work, and she proceeds to opens his pants and massage his privates.

After a minute of vigorous rubbing, she said, "Does that feel better?"

The player replies, "Yes, thank you. But I think you broke my thumb."

God and Golf

Toronto Maple Leafs General Manager Brian Burke and a priest are playing a friendly game of golf. Burke takes his first shot, misses and says, "Jesus! Dammit! I missed."

The priest is shocked and warns the foul-mouthed Burke, "Don't use that kind of language, or God will punish you."

On his next shot, Burke misses again and under his breath whispers, "Jesus Christ!"

The priest overhears him and says, "My son, please refrain from blasphemy, or God will surely punish you."

Burke, never one to sensor himself, approaches the ball, takes his shot, misses again and without pause says, "Jesus H. Christ, I missed again!"

Suddenly a bolt of lightning strikes the priest, killing him instantly. A voice from the heavens booms forth, "Jesus! Missed again!"

Three Wishes

A man was strolling along a river area in Chicago when he spotted a bottle floating in the water. The bottle drifted ashore, and he picked it up and opened it. Out popped a genie. "Master, you have released me from my bondage in this bottle. In exchange for my freedom, ask any three wishes, and I will grant them to you."

The man thought for a moment and said, "I would like the following three things to happen this year. The Chicago Cubs win the World Series, the Chicago Bulls win the NBA title and Chicago Blackhawks win the Stanley Cup."

The genie thought about this for a moment then jumped back into the bottle.

Season Tickets

Darlene was watching television in the living room with her husband, who was quietly reading a book.

"Sweetheart," she said. "Did you hear the story of the guy from Long Island who swapped his wife for a season's pass to the Islanders games? Would you give me up for anything like that?"

"Now, why would I go and do a stupid thing like that," he replied. "The season's half over."

The Leafs Defined

The Toronto Maple Leafs are a professional golf squad. Also known as the "Toronto Make-Me-Laffs," "Toronto Make Beliefs" and "Toronto Maple Loafs," the Leafs are known for their skilled antics, both on and off the course. Some of these activities include the breaststroke, hide-'n'-go-seek, tag, making "vroom" sounds while pretending to hold a steering wheel and calling the goalie "silly" after being scored on.

Poor San Jose Wife

A wife was having an affair with the TV repairman. She complained to him: "My husband never pays any attention to me. All he's ever bothered about is watching the latest San Jose Sharks game on TV. That's why we've got the biggest HDTV in the city— so he can watch all the games."

Just as she was telling this to the repairman, she heard the key in the front door. Her husband had arrived home early from work unexpectedly! She said to her lover, "Quick, hide behind the TV."

So the repairman hid behind the TV, while the husband got a beer and sat down to watch the hockey game. After half an hour, it became painful to stand behind the television, so the repairman simply walked straight past the husband and out the front door.

The husband turned to his wife and said: "Hey, honey, I didn't see the referee send that guy off, did you?"

Wild Manager

The Minnesota Wild manager won't stand for any nonsense. Last Saturday, he caught a couple of fans sneaking past security. He was furious. He grabbed them by the collars and said, "Now you just get back in there and watch the game until it finishes."

Washington Boys

Two inner-city Washington boys were playing with a new hockey net in the park near their house.

"Hey," shouted their mother, "where did you get that net?"

"We found it," replied one of the boys.

"Are you sure it was lost?" asked the mother curiously.

"Yes," replied the boy. "We saw some people looking for it just awhile ago."

Atlanta Game

One day, when the Thrashers were playing, the referee didn't turn up, so the coach asked if anyone among the spectators had refereeing experience. A man stepped forward.

"Have you refereed before?" asked the coach.

"Certainly," said the man. "And if you don't believe me, ask my three friends here."

"I'm sorry," said the coach. "But I don't think we can use you."

"Why not?"

"You can't be a real referee, because no real referee has three friends."

Dwarfs

The Seven Dwarfs got trapped in a mineshaft. Snow White ran to the entrance and yelled down to them. In the dark void, a voice called back, "Tampa Bay Lightning will win the Stanley Cup in 2012."

Snow White sighed. "Thank god! At least Dopey is still alive!"

Math Lessons

The Carolina Hurricanes coach walked into the locker room before a big game, looked over his star player and said, "I'm not supposed to let you play, since you failed math, but we really need you in there. So, what I have to do is ask you a math question, and if you get it right, you can play."

The player agreed, so the coach looked into his players eyes and asked, "Okay, now concentrate hard and tell me the answer to this: What is two plus two?"

The player thought hard for a moment and then answered, "four?"

"Did you say four?" asked the coach.

Suddenly, all the other players on the team began screaming, "Come on, Coach, give him another chance!"

Murder

Three fans are walking to GM Place for a Canucks-Maple Leafs hockey game, when they see a foot sticking out of some bushes. An inspection reveals a dead-drunk, naked woman. One man places his Rangers cap on her right breast. The Canucks fan places his cap on her left breast, and the Maple Leafs fan puts his over her crotch. They then call the police.

The cop lifts up the Rangers cap and makes a few notes. He then lifts the Canucks cap and makes a few more. Then he lifts the Maple Leaf cap, puts it down, lifts it again and puts it down. When he lifts it the third time, the Maple Leafs fan says, "What are you doing? Are you some kind of pervert, or what?"

The cop replies, "I'm just confused. Usually when I see a Maple Leafs cap, there's an asshole under it."

The Columbus Blue Jackets are going to the play-offs for the first time in franchise history. And no one is happier than the team's fan.

The captain of the Scranton Penguins was caught running naked through town. It's the first interesting thing to happen to Scranton since *The Office*. It's also the most indecent thing to happen in Pennsylvania since the Pirates. The player has since been charged with public drunkenness, disorderly conduct, open lewdness and high sticking.

Oh, Those Ducks Fans

So, a Ducks fan walks into a sports store in Ottawa and asks, "Do you have any Anaheim T-shirts?"

The clerk replies, "No, of course not! This is an Ottawa sporting goods store, and we don't sell Anaheim T-shirts! Now get the hell out of here!"

So, the Ducks fan comes back the next day and asks again, "Do you have any Anaheim T-shirts?"

The clerk says, "I told you before: NO, I don't have any! Now leave!"

So the Ducks fan comes back the next day and asks, "Do you have any Anaheim T-shirts?"

The angry clerk says, "I told you! NO! And if you come back and ask me that again, I will nail your butt to the wall! Now leave!"

So, the Ducks fan comes back the next day and asks, "Do you have any nails?"

The clerk, who was really angry now but at the same time puzzled, says, "NO, YOU IDIOT! This is a sports store. Why do you think I would have nails?"

The Ducks fan says, "In that case, do you have any Anaheim T-shirts?"

More Genies

A Red Wings fan and a Predators fan were walking one day and found a bottle. The Predators fan picked it up, and a genie appeared. The genie said he would grant each a wish that would benefit the city of their favourite team. He asked the Red Wings fan first.

"Seeing how we've won two Stanley Cups recently and are so much better than anybody else," the fan said, "I would like to have a wall around Detroit, so that we don't have to associate with those of lower stature."

The genie granted his request. He then asked the Predators fan for his wish to benefit the city of Nashville.

The Predators fan thought a minute and then said to the genie, "Tell me about that wall."

The genie replied, "The wall is 150 feet tall, 50 feet thick and totally indestructible."

The Predators fan then said, "Fill that baby up with water."

Counting

One day, this guy is sitting in a bar having a drink. Suddenly, he's startled by three Ottawa Senators hockey players cheering, "Fifteen! Fifteen!" He ignores them and continues to drink.

About five minutes later, the hockey players again cheer, "Fifteen! Fifteen!"

At this, the guy walks over and asks them why they keep cheering.

The hockey players respond, "Well, we went to Wal-mart and bought this jigsaw puzzle. We put it together in 15 weeks, and we're excited because the side of the box said it'd take 3–5 years."

Exhausted

An exhausted-looking Montréal Canadiens fan dragged himself into the doctor's office. "Doctor, there are dogs all over my neighbourhood. They bark all day and all night, and I can't get a wink of sleep."

"I have good news for you," the doctor answered, rummaging through a drawer full of sample medications. "Here are some new sleeping pills that work like a dream. A few of these and your troubles will be over."

"Great," the Canadiens fan answered. "I'll try anything. Let's give it a shot."

A few weeks later the Canadiens fan returned, looking worse than ever. "Doc, your plan is no good. I'm more tired than before!"

"I don't understand how that could be," said the doctor, shaking his head. "Those are the strongest pills on the market!"

"That may be true," answered the Canadiens fan wearily, "but I'm still up all night chasing those dogs, and when I do finally catch one, it's just about impossible to get him to swallow the damn pill!"

Fire! Fire!

There was a huge fire at the All-Star game. Three hockey fans, each wearing the jersey of their favourite teams, were stranded on the roof. One was a Canadiens fan, one a Leafs fan and the last a Senators fan.

The fire department came with a blanket and yelled to the Canadiens fan to jump. He jumped, and they moved the blanket to the right. He hit the sidewalk with a splat.

Then they called to the Toronto fan to jump. He said that he wouldn't jump. The firemen explained that they hated the Canadiens. The fan said he hated them, too, and jumped. Again, the fire department moved the blanket to the right, and the fan hit the ground with a splat.

Finally, they called to the Senators fan to jump. He said that he wouldn't jump. The fire department said they really hated the Leafs.

He yelled back, "I don't trust you. Lay the blanket down, and then I'll jump!"

Dear Ann Landers,

I have a problem. I have two brothers. One lives in Québec and is an avid supporter of the Montréal Canadiens. My other brother has just been sentenced to death in the electric chair in Florida.

My two sisters are both prostitutes, and my father deals narcotics.

Recently I met a woman who was just released from prison, where she served time for smothering her illegitimate child. I want to marry this woman. My problem is: If I marry this woman, should I tell her about my brother who is the Montréal Canadiens fan?

Florida Panthers Mission Statement

Our team lives hockey

It dreams hockey

It eats hockey

Now, if it could only play hockey.

A man from New Jersey moved to New York. As he wandered the streets, he stopped at an antique shop and decided to go in. After looking around, he noticed a strange bronze cat with a tag on it saying, "Bronze Cat $30.00, Story $150.00." The man was very curious and asked the salesman to explain.

"Well" said the man, "it's just like it says: $30 for the cat and $150 for its story."

"I'll just take the cat," said the man.

"Okay, but you will be back," said the salesman.

The man left the shop with the cat in his pocket. As he walked down the street, he heard a strange mewing sound. There were a couple of cats following him. The farther he walked, the more cats seemed to follow him. As he got to the Brooklyn Bridge, he turned to see thousands of cats behind him.

"Screw this!" he said to himself and threw the bronze cat into the river. All the cats jumped into the river, too, and were drowned. The man returned to the shop where he bought the cat.

"I knew you would be back—$150.00 for the story," said the salesman.

"Forget the story," said the man. "Have you got a bronze Rangers fan?"

How Teams Can Improve Attendance!

Anaheim Mighty Ducks

Require players to change their jersey names to recognized Walt Disney characters such as Goofy, Grumpy, Cinderella and Dumbo.

Boston Bruins

All the Sam Adams you can drink for $10! Any fan wearing the traditional Bostonian uniform of work boots, blue jeans, turtleneck sweater and baseball cap pays $5.

Buffalo Sabres

Change the team name to the "Buffalo Wet T-Shirt Contest" for a night, so they will finally attract some attention from the rest of the league.

Calgary Flames

Both the players and the fans will now wear paper bags with cut-out eyes and mouth holes, so no one will recognize them.

Carolina Hurricanes

Tractor pulls during the first intermission, dirt-bike racing during the second.

Chicago Blackhawks

One fan per game gets to select a team identity, and the Blackhawks must play under the chosen identity for that game.

Colorado Avalanche

All Avalanche management and their wives will appear at games wearing barrels or potato sacks and holding tin cups. They will then proceed to walk around the arena and hand out little cards that say, "We are now destitute because we wanted you, our darling fans, to keep your number one centre, Joe Sakic."

Dallas Stars

The players will now wear football helmets in place of hockey helmets, and a regulation NFL football will replace the puck for home games. Might as well try it. Things can't get any worse.

Detroit Red Wings

Change arena name from "Joe Louis Arena" to "Claude Lemieux Sucks Arena."

Edmonton Oilers
Require players to wear "Classic Oiler" jerseys with legendary Oiler names and numbers on the back instead of their own.

Florida Panthers
Permit fans to throw whatever objects they bring with them onto the ice.

Los Angeles Kings
Plan on folding the team and turning the arena into a trendy nightclub.

Montréal Canadiens
Management promises to acquire every player in the league with a French-Canadian name.

Nashville Predators
"Fire a Puck at the Country-and-Western Singer of Your Choice" game during intermission!

New Jersey Devils
Any fan caught uttering a complaint against The Royal Order of the New Jersey Devils or its management will be traded to Edmonton or San Jose.

New York Islanders
Remote tropical island getaway theme. Fake palm trees scattered about the arena, sounds of waves and seagulls broadcast over the PA system. Every fan receives a flower lei upon entering.

New York Rangers

Centre ice scoreboard now solely devoted to the latest NYSE and NASDAQ stock quotes. The team's name will also be changed to RnGr +3-1/4.

Ottawa Senators

Schedule "Hall of Fame" games pitting 1990s Senators against original 1920s Ottawa Senators.

Philadelphia Flyers

"Play Goal For Us 2-Nite!" fan lottery before every home game.

Phoenix Coyotes

Every fan receives a copy of the "Tommy and Pamela Lee" home video on entry.

Pittsburgh Penguins

In the spirit of the Penguins "colourful" play-by-play announcer, rented mules will actually be beaten at centre-ice after each Jagr goal.

San Jose Sharks

No changes necessary. They've been packing them in for years, despite having lousy teams.

St. Louis Blues

A colour photo of Mike Keenan, smiling, will be placed in every urinal before game time.

Tampa Bay Lightning

One lucky fan per game will be struck by lightning generated by the centre-ice scoreboard.

Toronto Maple Leafs

Separate from the rest of the "Americanized" NHL and form own league, in which the Toronto Maple Leafs play the Toronto Maple Leafs every night.

Vancouver Canucks

Hand out bricks and tire irons to fans as they exit to aid them in their post-game riots.

Washington Capitals

Any fan who can explain the concept of off-sides or a delayed penalty receives two free season tickets.

Chapter Ten

Dumping Ground

I Smart

Half an hour before practice, a player walks into the medical room and says, "Doc I hurt all over."

Even though it was the doctor's first day on the job, he was not naïve enough to believe him. So the doctor says, "That's impossible. You're just trying to get the day off, right?"

"No, really, I hurt all over," the player insists. "Look, when I touch my arm, ouch. When I touch my leg, ouch. When I touch my chest, ouch. When I touch my head, ouch."

The doctor just nods and asks, "You've had more than 10 concussions, haven't you?"

The player looks puzzled and then says, "Yes, how did you know?"

The doctor replies, "Because your finger is broken."

What Daddy Does?

Johnny was in his fifth-grade class, when the teacher asked the children what their fathers did for a living. All the typical answers came up: fireman, policeman, salesman. Johnny was being uncharacteristically quiet, so the teacher asked him about his father. Johnny said, "My father is an exotic dancer at a gay bar and takes all his clothes off in front of other men. Sometimes, if the offer's really good, he'll go out to the alley with some guy and have sex with him for money."

The teacher, obviously shaken by his statement, hurriedly set the other children to work on some colouring and took Johnny aside to ask him, "Is that really true about your father?"

"Well, not really" said Johnny. "He plays for the Phoenix Coyotes, but I was too embarrassed to say that in front of the other kids."

A Boy and His Mom

Mom: Was there a fight at the game today? You've lost your front teeth.

Son: No, I haven't. They're in my pocket.

Finding His Place

On his way back from the concession stand at the Bell Centre, Pierre asked a man at the end of the row, "Pardon moi, but did I step on your foot a few minutes ago?"

Expecting an apology, the man said, "Indeed, you did."

Pierre nodded and said, "Oh good. Then this is my row."

Daddy Daddy!

Little Johnny arrived home after his hockey game, threw open the door and ran to his Dad, who had been unable to attend the game.

"How was the game, son? How did you do?" asked his father.

"You aren't going to believe it, Dad!" Johnny exclaimed. "I was responsible for the winning goal!"

"That's wonderful," his Dad said. "How did you do that?"

"I missed my check on the other team's high scorer!"

Young Hockey

At one point during a game, the coach called one of his seven-year-old hockey players aside and asked, "Do you understand what co-operation is? What a team is?"

The little boy nodded in the affirmative.

"Do you understand that what matters is not whether we win or lose but how we play together as a team?"

The little boy nodded yes.

The coach continued, "I am sure you know, when a penalty is called, that you should not argue, curse, attack the referee or call him a bloody idiot. Do you understand all that?"

Again the little boy nodded.

"And when I call you off the ice so that another boy gets a chance to play, it's not good sportsmanship to call your coach a dumb jackass, is it?"

The little boy shook his head no.

"Good," said the coach. "Now go over there and explain all that to your mother...."

TV Problem

Larry came to work one day, limping something awful. One of his co-workers, Joe, noticed and asked Larry what happened.

Larry replied, "Oh nothing. It's just an old hockey injury that acts up once in a while."

Joe said, "Gee, I never knew you played hockey."

Larry said, "Oh, I don't play. I hurt it last year when I lost $100 on the Stanley Cup playoffs. I got mad and put my foot through the television."

Mammals Versus Insects

A team of mammals was playing a team of insects. The mammals totally dominated the first and second period and were leading 28–0. However, in the second intermission, the insects made a substitution and brought on a centipede. The centipede scored an incredible 200 goals in the third period, and the insects won the game by a final score of 200–28.

Afterward, in the dressing room, the captain of the mammals was chatting to the insect captain. "That centipede of yours is terrific," the mammals captain said. "Why didn't you play him from the start?"

"We'd have liked to," said the insect captain. "But it takes him 45 minutes to get his skates on."

Doctor!

After only a few games playing for the Montréal Canadiens, the new goalkeeper had already let in 10 goals. He was having a drink in a bar one night, when a man approached him and asked, "I've been watching you play, and I think I might be able to help you."

"Are you a trainer?" said the poor Canadiens goalkeeper.

"No," said the stranger. "I'm an optician."

Poor Thing

Patricia began her job in a secondary school as a counsellor, and she was keen to help the pupils. One day during break time, she noticed a girl standing all by herself at one end of the hockey rink, while the rest of the children were enjoying a game of hockey at the other end. Patricia approached and asked if she was all right. The girl said that she was.

Some time later, however, Patricia noticed that the girl was in exactly the same spot, still by herself. Going up to her again, she inquired, "Would you like me to be your friend?"

The girl hesitated, then said, "All right." But she looked at Patricia suspiciously.

Feeling she was making progress, Patricia then asked, "Why are you standing here all alone?"

"Because," the girl said with a big sigh. "I'm the goalie!"

Oh, Girl!

A hockey fan took his new girlfriend to a game for the first time and answered all her questions as she inquired about the role of every player.

"And what's that man in front of the net?" she asked.

"He's the goalkeeper," he said.

"And what does he do?" she asked.

"He has to keep the puck from going in the net."

"Ah. And how much is he paid?" she asked again.

"Oh, about $10,000 a week."

"Oh," said the girl. "Wouldn't it be cheaper to board it up?"

Intense Hockey Fans

Two hockey fans were in court for fighting. One fan had bitten off part of the other's ear, and the judge told him he was fined $600.

"But it was self-defence," he complained.

The judge ignored him. "You're fined $600 and bound to keep the peace for a year."

"I can't do that," said the fan. "I threw it in a dustbin."

Delivery

A married couple go to hospital together to have their baby delivered. When they arrive, the doctor says they have just taken delivery of a new machine that transfers a portion of the mother's pain to the father.

"Would you be willing to try it out?" asks the doctor.

"Yes, of course," says the husband, who is very much a Sensitive, New Age Guy.

As the woman goes into labour, the doctor sets the machine to 10 percent and asks the man if it hurts. "No, it's fine," he says. The doctor raises the setting to 20 percent. "Still okay," says the man. The doctor gradually lifts the setting to 50 percent. The husband closes his eyes and grits his teeth but insists he can cope without any problem. So the doctor raises it gradually to 75 percent.

"I can take it," says the husband. "Give me the full 100 percent." So the doctor does, and the wife bears the baby with no pain at all.

The doctor goes off to write up the case for a medical journal, while the couple takes their baby home. On the doorstep, they find their 10-year-old son's hockey coach dead.

Hockey Tournament Weekend

Four married guys went away on a hockey tournament weekend. On their first day out, they began talking about the trouble they had getting permission from their wives to go away.

The first guy said, "I had so much trouble getting away. I had to promise my wife I'd paint the whole house."

The second chimed in and said, " Oh yeah! I had to promise my wife I'll go shopping with her next weekend."

The third laughed. "That's nothing. I had to promise my wife I'd let her mother stay for a whole week."

The fourth guy snickered. "It was no problem for me. I just set the alarm to go off at 5:30 this morning. When it went off, I gave my wife a poke and said, "Hockey tournament or sex?" And she said, 'Don't forget your skates.'"

What a Woman!

A retired corporate executive, now a widower, decides to take a vacation. He books himself on a Caribbean cruise and proceeds to have the time of his life, until, one day, the ship sinks. He finds himself on an island with no other people and no supplies. He is forced to live on bananas and coconuts.

After about four months, he is lying on the beach, when the most gorgeous woman he has ever seen rows up to the shore.

In disbelief, he asks, "Where did you come from? How did you get here?" She replies, "I rowed from the other side of the island. I landed here when my cruise ship sank."

"Amazing," he notes. "You were really lucky to have a row boat wash up with you."

"Oh, this thing?" explains the woman. "I made the boat out of raw material I found on the island. The oars were whittled from gum tree branches. I wove the bottom from palm branches, and the sides and stern came from a eucalyptus tree."

"But, where did you get the tools?"

"Oh, that was no problem," replied the woman. "On the south side of the island, a very unusual stratum of alluvial rock is exposed. I found if I fired it to a certain temperature in my kiln, it melted into ductile iron. I used that for tools and used the tools to make the hardware."

The guy is stunned.

"Let's row over to my place," she says.

After a few minutes of rowing, she docks the boat at a small wharf. As the man looks to shore, he nearly falls off the boat. Before him is a stone walk leading to an exquisite bungalow painted in blue and white.

While the woman ties up the rowboat with an expertly woven hemp rope, the man can only stare ahead, dumbstruck. As they walk into the house, she says casually, "It's not much, but I call it home. Sit down, please. Would you like a drink?"

"No! No thank you," he blurts out, still dazed. "I can't take another drop of coconut juice."

"It's not coconut juice," winks the woman. "I have a still. How would you like a piña colada?"

Trying to hide his continued amazement, the man accepts, and they sit down on her couch to talk. After they have exchanged their stories, the woman announces, "I'm going to slip into something more comfortable. Would you like to take a shower and shave? There is a razor upstairs in the bathroom cabinet."

No longer questioning anything, the man goes into the bathroom. There, in the cabinet, he finds a razor made from a piece of tortoise bone. Two shells honed to a hollow ground edge are fastened onto its end inside a swivel mechanism.

"This woman is amazing," he muses. "What next?"

When he returns, she greets him wearing nothing but strategically positioned vines and smelling faintly of gardenias. She beckons for him to sit down next to her.

"Tell me," she begins suggestively, slithering closer to him. "We've been out here for many months. You've been lonely. Surely there's something you've missed, something you feel like doing right now, something you've longed for terribly?"

She stares into his eyes. The man looks back, bewildered. He can't believe what he's hearing. "You mean," he begins, swallowing excitedly, tears filling his eyes, "you mean, you've built a hockey rink?!"

Hit Man

A group of friends played hockey at the local out-door arena every Saturday. One Saturday, they were getting ready to play, when a strange guy asked them if he could join in. The friends looked at each other and then looked at the man and said it was okay. So, they started to play.

About 20 minutes into the game, the friends were pretty curious about the man and asked him what he did for a living. The stranger told them that he was a hit man. The friends laughed, and the man said, "No really, I am a hit man. My gun is in my hockey bag. I carry it everywhere I go. You can take a look if you like."

So, one of the guys decided he would. He opened up the bag, and, sure enough, it held a rifle with a huge scope on it. Excited, he said, "Wow! I bet I can see my house through here! May I look?"

The stranger handed him the rifle. The man looked for a second and said, "You can! I can even see through my windows into my bedroom. There's my wife, naked. Isn't she beautiful? Wait! There's my next door neighbour! And he's naked too!"

This upset the man, so he asked the hit man how much it would be for a hit.

The hit man replied, "It's $1000 every time I pull the trigger."

The man said, "$1000, ouch! Still, I want two hits. Shoot my wife right in the mouth. She is always nagging at me, and I can't stand it. Then shoot my neighbour right in the dick, just for screwing around with my wife."

The hit man gears up and looks through the scope. After about five minutes, the man starts to get impatient and asks the hit man what he is waiting for.

The hitman replies, "If you'll hold on for a minute, I'll save you a thousand bucks."

Christmas

A father asked his son what he'd like for Christmas. "I've got my eye on these special goalie pads in the sports store window," replied the young lad.

"The $900 ones?" asked the father.

"That's right."

"Well keep your eye on them all you want, but you're never gonna play in them," said dad firmly.

Dumb Kid

A huge University of Alberta freshman figured he'd try out for the hockey team. "Can you check?" asked the coach.

"Watch this," said the freshman, who proceeded to speed into a defenseman, shattering the glass in the boards to smithereens.

"Wow," said the coach. "I'm impressed. Can you skate fast?"

"Of course I can skate," said the freshman. He was off like a shot, and, in just over nine seconds, he had skated around the rink.

"Great!" enthused the coach. "But can you pass a puck?"

The freshman rolled his eyes, hesitated for a few seconds. "Well, sir," he said. "I guess if I can manage to swallow it, I can probably pass it."

Lettuce Head

A man walked into the produce section of his local supermarket and asked to buy half a head of lettuce. The boy working in that department told him that they only sold whole heads of lettuce.

The man insisted that the boy ask his manager about the matter. Walking into the back room, the boy said to his manager, "Some a-hole wants to buy half a head of lettuce." As he finished his sentence, he turned to find the man standing right behind him. So he added, "And this gentleman kindly offered to buy the other half."

The manager approved the deal, and the man went on his way.

Later, the manager found the boy and said "I was impressed with the way you got yourself out of that situation earlier. We like people who think on their feet here. Where are you from, son?"

"Canada, sir" the boy replied.

"Well, why did you leave Canada," the manager asked.

The boy said "Sir, there's nothing but whores and hockey players up there."

"Really!" the manager said angrily. "My wife is from Canada."

The boy replied, "No kidding? Who did she play for?"

Hockey Wife

A hockey wife was complaining about her husband spending all his free time at the clubhouse with the rest of the team after matches.

So, one Saturday after the match, he took her along with him. "What'll you have?" he asked.

"Oh, I don't know. The same as you, I suppose," she replied.

So, the husband ordered a couple of Grouse and threw his down in one shot.

His wife watched him then took a sip from her glass and immediately spat it out.

"Yuck, that's *terrible*!" she spluttered. "I don't know how you can drink this stuff!"

"Well, there you go," cried the husband. "And you think I'm out enjoying myself!"

Three Sports

There were three sports players: a football player, a tennis player and a hockey player. The football player checked into a hotel, but, when he got to his room, he heard, "I am the ghost of Meanie-enie. I am going to eat your weenie!" The football player checked out really fast.

Then the tennis player went to the same hotel and got the same room. The same thing happened to him, and he checked out really fast, too.

Finally, the hockey player went to the hotel and got the same room. When he heard, "I am the ghost of Meanie-enie. I am going to eat your weenie!" he said, "Touch my weenie, I kick your ass."

Q: How many inline hockey players does it take to screw in a light bulb?

A: None. They're all so "brilliant," they don't need light bulbs!

Two old hockey players—a centre and a goalie—made a deal with each other. The first one to pass away would tell the other if there was hockey in heaven.

The centre was the first to pass away. Two weeks later, as the old goalie was watching a game, a vision of his friend appeared above the television.

"Well?" asked the goalie. "Is there hockey in heaven?"

"Yes," smiled the ghost.

"That's fantastic!" the old goalie shouted, jumping up.

"But I have some bad news," said his ghost friend.

"Bad news? What bad news?"

"Well," said the ghost. "You're starting in net tomorrow."

Coaches

There are three hockey coaches. One is young, one is middle-aged, one is older. They discuss the way they call a play.

The young coach brags, "I call it the way it is."

The middle-aged coach brags, "I call it the way I see it."

The older coach says, "It's nothing till I call it."

They say there are three ways to play hockey: rough, rougher and "I'll help you find your teeth, if you'll help me look for mine."

Hockey Language Glossary

Spanish

English		
Hockey	el hockey sobre heilo	ehl hockey so-bray high-loh
Puck	disco de caucho	dee-skoh day kow-choh
Goal!	meta! or porteria!	may-tah or por-teh-reeo
Forward	delantero	day-lahn-tay-roh
Defenceman	campeon	kahm-pay-oh
Goaltender	guardameta	gwah-dah-may-tah

Czech

English		
Hockey	hokej	hoh-kyay
Puck	puk	puck
Goal!	gol/branka!	gohl/(brahn-kah)
Forward	utocnik	ooh-toe-sneek

| Defenceman | obrance or pravni | oh-bran-chay or prahv-nee |
| Goaltender | brankar | brahn-kaar* |

Swedish

Hockey	ishockey	eyes-hoh-key
Puck	puck	puhk
Goal!	göra mal!	gueh-rrah mahl
Forward	anfallsspelare	ahn-fohl-speh-lah-rey
Defenceman	försvarsspelare	feuhrs-vehs-pey-lah-rey
Goaltender	målvakt	mohl-vekt

German

Hockey	Eishockey	ice-hockey
Puck	die scheibe	dee sh-eye-beh
Goal!	Tor!	tohr
Forward	Sturm	sh-toorm
Defenceman	Verteidiger	vehr-tye-diger
Goaltender	der Torwart	tohr-wahrt

Finnish

Hockey	Jääkiekko	*yah-kiec*-oh
Puck	Kiekko	*kiec*-oh
Goal!	Maali!	*maah*-lih

Forward	Hyökkääjä	*hyoc*-ka-ya
Defenceman	Puolustaja	*puoh*-lush-taya
Goaltender	Maalivahti	*mah*-liv-ahti

French

Hockey	l'Hockey sur glace	hoh-kee syur glah-ss
Puck	le palet/la rondelle	pah-lay/ Rohn-dell
Goal!	Marqué!/Buts!	mar-kay/Byoo
Forward	l'Avant	ah-van
Defenceman	le Defenseur	deu-fahn-syoo
Goaltender	le Gardien	gahr-dee-yen

Italian

Hockey	hockey	*whoa*-kay
Puck	disco bella	dee-sko *bell*-uh
Goal!	meta!	*may*-tuh
Forward	avanti	ah-*vahn*-ti
Defenceman	difensore	dee-fen-*sore*-eh
Goaltender	portière	*por*-tee-air-eh

*These terms are more often associated with soccer. When speaking of hockey in Italy, you specify "hockey player" as *hockeista* or *discatore* (literally, "puck-mover"). For example, a soccer fullback is merely a *difensore*, but a defender on a hockey blue line would be noted by the complete term *hockheista difensore*.

Canadian

Hockey	HOCKEY	haw-kee
Puck	biscuit	bis-kit
Goal!	Nirvana!	nir-vah-na
Forward	Oldest Child	(family term)
Defenceman	Middle Child	(family term)
Goaltender	Youngest Child	(family term)

Notes on Sources

www.anecdotage.com/index.php?aid=1924

sports.yahoo.com/nhl/blog/puck_daddy/post/Hockey-mystery-What-happens-to-hats-thrown-for-?urn=nhl,167824

www.angelfire.com/rant/leeaf83/hockeyhumour.html

www.hhof.com/html/humour.shtml

uncyclopedia.wikia.com/wiki/Stanley_Cup

www.thehockeynews.com/forum/viewtopic.php?f=5&t=80&st=0&sk=t&sd=a&sid=ce05b70207ecdfb35091e7b90dc8c8b2&start=50

ohiochill.tripod.com/HamptonRoadsAdmirals/id18.html

www.contestcen.com/jokes3.htm

www.indefual.net/canada/jokes/mb-cnd.html

www.indefual.net/canada/jokes/index.html

www.canadaka.net/

www.ahajokes.com/eng007.html

J. Alexander Poulton

J. Alexander Poulton is a writer, photographer and genuine Canadian sports enthusiast. A resident of Montréal all his life, he has been know to "call in sick" during the broadcasts of major sports events so that he can get as much viewing in as possible.

He earned his B.A. in English literature from McGill University and his graduate diploma in journalism from Concordia University. He has 15 other sports books to his credit, including books on hockey, soccer, curling and the Olympics.